Living Your Legacy:

Change Your Story, Impact Your World,

and Become a Visionary Leader

Sharon Olson

Living Your Legacy Copyright © 2017 Sharon Olson

All rights reserved. No part of this publication may be reproduced, distributed, or transmitted in any form or by any means, including photocopying, recording, or other electronic or mechanical methods, without the prior written permission of the publisher, except in the case of brief quotations embodied in reviews and certain other non-commercial uses permitted by copyright law.

ISBN: 1537734709

ISBN-13: 978-1537734705

To LeRoy
I wouldn't be where I am today if it weren't for the legacy of love you live every day.

I also dedicate this book to the giants who have helped me stand on their shoulders.
Your legacies demonstrate the power of living a generous story, impacting generations, and leading cultures of honor.
Thank you for your investment in me.

And to the reader, I dedicate this book to you.
I'm honored to be on this adventure with you.

Table of Contents

Foreword 7

Introduction 9

Section 1
Change Your Story

1 This Is Bigger Than Us 17

Vision:

2 Crafting Your Legacy 45

3 Identity Leads the Storyline 65

4 The Power of A Tenacious Vocabulary 91

Section 2
Impact Your World

5 A Culture of Accountability 100

6 A Culture of Exploration 126

Section 3
Become A Visionary Leader

7 The Legacy of A Community 144

8 Always Be On Mission 169

9 Transformational and Empowering Leadership 190

Conclusion 212

Acknowledgments 221

About the Author 230

Foreword

We often hear about leaving a legacy. We all want that, in some way, I suppose. Sports stars, entertainers, and business moguls are prime candidates for leaving a legacy. But what about the rest of us? Leaders throw it out there for us to think about. But it's the rare speaker, author, or coach who shows us how to leave a legacy. Rarer still? A visionary leader who shows us how to live a legacy. Sharon Olson does exactly that.

Living Your Legacy is a book unlike any I've ever read. It will get you planning a vision greater than yourself. It will inspire you with stories of ordinary greatness. And it will give you tools to live your legacy now, not to wait and leave a legacy when you're gone.

I'm drawn to big-idea people, big thinkers who look at the world and ask, "How am I going to make my mark?" Sharon Olson is one of those people, and I'm glad I had the good fortune to meet her a couple years ago. As a business coach, I help authors, bloggers, and copywriters market themselves. Usually we discuss things like platform, positioning, and personal branding.

Sharon and I talked about those things on our very first Skype call between Madison, Wisconsin, and Ramstein, Germany. Then we quickly went much deeper. "We get one shot at this life," she told me, and it still echoes in my ear. She wants to do life on a grand scale and live a purposeful life. Sharon envisions meeting with world leaders and celebrities. Not as a star-struck admirer, but as someone who can help them live their legacy.

I have no doubt she will, and I have no doubt she'll help you live your legacy. She's already doing it with friends, clients, colleagues . . . and her children. Sharon and her husband, LeRoy, have taught their three sons and a daughter to be world-changers, and they're well on their way. You will be, too, when you finish this book.

Don't wait until you're dead to leave a legacy. Live your legacy. Now. Change your story, impact your world, and become a visionary leader. Sharon will fill you in on the details.

—Steve Roller
Founder and Publisher of CafeWriter.com

INTRODUCTION

The ten of us stood there swatting at the occasional fly. Beads of sweat slid down the nape of my neck. Thin notebooks on a table leaned against the wall as though someone had pulled one from the bottom of the pile, then hurried away before arranging them neatly again. Their brown covers, with a space for Name, Subject, and Period, spoke of simple sophistication. Like something out of a high-end department store whose customers were enamored by the romance of earthy products made from recycled materials.

The fragrance of sun-dried clothes mingled with dirt and sweat. Though not unpleasant, future experiences would elicit the comment, "The smell in here is like the African Bush."

"Do you have any questions for us?" Our host smiled as she asked the question, her expression willing us to get on with the informal interview. No fewer than 300 children watched us through the screen door, their pushing and shoving to get a closer look kept at bay only by an occasional shout from a teacher. Five teachers for almost 800 children. Over 200 children filled the kindergarten alone, each class size smaller as they progressed through the twelfth grade.

I looked intently into the eyes of one of the teachers. His pants cuffs hovered an inch or so above thin, bony ankles, the suit coat threadbare with a spot of dried mud on his left sleeve. His cheekbones accentuated large dark eyes with yellowish tinting where they should have been white.

"Are you who you dreamed of being? Is this the vision you had for your life?" The question bubbled up from an idealistic and unshakable optimism. After all, didn't everyone everywhere in the world *naturally* envision who they want to be and the legacy they want to live? However, enraptured by the scene playing out around me—in my view, a scene filled with possibility and amazement—my question lacked resonance. Dream? Vision? In a culture where an entire season every year is notorious for the "hunger season," such an inquiry ushered in the cultural dissonance I had hoped to avoid.

The stifling heat, combined with my lack of understanding, compressed the air in the room. The man glanced over at his colleagues, seeming to search for an answer that would satisfy a naïve, over-zealous American.

"The way it works here," he paused, his eyes holding my eyes intently, like he wanted to make sure he was getting through, "becoming a teacher is the best one can hope. It's the only work that makes enough money to live. I studied hard in school to take the exams—which are really hard to pass—and when I passed the exams, I became certified to teach. But it's still hard to find a job. So when I heard that they needed a teacher in Dzuwa, I applied and got work here. The government pays for my housing and it pays me a salary. It's not what I dreamed of doing. It's just the best I could do."

The other teachers nodded, smiling forgiveness. They understood something they hoped I might comprehend, too.

My heart beat hard and I wasn't sure if it was from the overwhelming sense of claustrophobia, standing in a space smaller than most people's closets back home, or the thought of walking back out to a throng of onlookers who pressed in with curiosity at the foreigners visiting their village.

"Well, then! Shall we move on? The teachers need to get back to their classes!" Our host gestured toward the door and one of the teachers pushed the screen open with a bit of effort against the crowd of raucous children. They shouted something in Chichewa and the children moved away, some of them running toward nearby buildings.

We visited the remaining classes, the spacious rooms sparsely furnished with desks and benches, the walls empty of graphics or decorations. Benches made for two accommodated three or four students to allow everyone a seat. A blackboard hung on the front wall and only one class had a podium on which the teacher placed his notebook while he taught.

The students sang for us—some of them obviously outgoing and excited to perform, while others smiled shyly with hands tucked in their laps, their shoulders stooped as they mouthed the words. But I couldn't shake the effects of the conversation only moments ago. I smiled, grateful, at the children as they sang, but I searched their faces. *Becoming a teacher is the best one can hope.* The teacher's words played on a continuous loop in my mind. I wondered what the students hoped for. It struck me how in their culture, education was a profound privilege. Despite their ill-fitted, frayed and faded uniforms, they somehow managed to acquire the required green and white attire. They listened, attentive and respectful, as the teachers spoke. They seemed to want to be there, acting as though something important and life-changing was taking place.

When I asked our host about my observation, she looked at me wide-eyed, "Yes. Of course. They know that getting a good education will make all the difference."

My thoughts flitted back to the educational paradigm in America, where every young person is entitled to an education in the first twelve grades. Where in middle school and high school, a guidance or career counselor meets with students to ask what they want to do when they grow up. How they tailor dreams in with required classes. And I thought about how much I took for granted. How somewhere along the way, I took *hope* for granted.

I thought back to the moment when I asked the teacher if he was living his vision, wanting to take it back and tell him instead, *Thank you. For investing your life into these children. Thank you for being a leader and role model. Thank you for choosing to develop your students' potential. For giving them hope. For choosing* this *as your legacy.*

Unnerved and unsettled, I felt like a spoiled aristocrat. Bourgeoisie of the Bush.

I couldn't shake it. More than ever, I felt the ridiculous privilege—rather, responsibility—to steward my legacy. To live a more passionate, intentional, and service-minded legacy, invested in helping others live wholehearted, hope-filled lives. I thought about the leaders in my life who had come alongside me in the roles of teachers, counselors, mentors, and coaches. How, because of their influence, they opened whole worlds of opportunities to me.

Is there any legacy greater or richer than showing up for our lives right where we are, in the best way we know, and then helping others see the inestimable value of their lives, too? That they are worthy of hopes and dreams. Of love and belonging. That they have influence and can make a difference.

I used to think I wanted to give a voice to those who need a voice. And while I believe there's a time and place for that, now I know I want to teach and coach people to find *their voice* and to use it to make a positive difference in the world.

Meeting Dzuwa's teachers and students poured a massive dose of fuel on an ever-growing vision for training, coaching, and mentoring leaders. To help people recognize the significance of their contribution to the world. We're not called to fix all the problems in the world. But we don't have any excuses to play small. To hold back. To not give everything we can to the spaces where we live and work. More than ever, that moment solidified for me the responsibility we *all* have to show up with a spirit of generosity. To love more fiercely and fearlessly. To inspire and cultivate hope.

Our lives are a stewardship. Too important to be haphazard or to settle for mediocrity.

There's a lot of people on this planet who show up, give extravagantly from what they have, and make the world a better place by bringing out the best in those around them. This book is a tribute to those people, those who make a difference where they are, with what they've been given.

This book is also a call-to-action to those who are comfortable, secure, and relatively happy. Now is not the time for complacency. You have more in you. More art. More music. More ideas. More love. More connection. More authority. More influence. More solutions. More adventure.

Humans are amazing. What difference might we make in the world if we all pressed hard into our best hope? What if we framed our stories with hope? Perhaps we might live out more of the amazing that's *already* inside us. Maybe we'd be a tiny bit more brave about bringing our creativity, connection, love, happiness, and ideas to the places where we live and work. Maybe we'd all be more fully present.

Life is really short. I'll reiterate this over and over in this book. I'm not trying to be morbid, but in the grand scheme of eternity, our lives fill the expanse of a vapor. So, here's the deal . . . if you're reading this, please know, you are loved. You belong here. The world needs your best hope, your vision, your leadership. The places where you live and work need the legacy you're living right now, today.

It's taken me way too long to live fully into the truth that I'm already enough. As you'll see in the pages ahead, I've learned (and am still learning) to stop spending so much time getting ready for my life and to instead invest this time into living a legacy full of passion, joy, hope, adventure, and love. To show up fully present and give myself grace to grow through life's inevitable lessons. As one of my mentors, Austin Netzley, is keen to say, "If you're fully prepared, you probably waited too long."

And by living our legacy in the present? By bringing our best hope right where we are? This is how we outlive our lives.

We may never fully comprehend the impact our lives make on those around us. A word of encouragement, a smile, the steady eye contact as we listen with rapt attention to another.

This book is a result of the interminable fascination I have with stories. Both our collective stories as well as the unique story of each of us. The fact that we all come into the world the same—naked. And then, the fact that no two stories are ever exactly the same? Well, it's perfectly astounding.

Who can predict the profound impact the teachers in Dzuwa have on their students? What hopes might be fostered and expanded? Who can predict the impact our stories—our leadership—might have on those around us?

I wouldn't be who I am today, a dreamer on a big adventure of learning what it means to live a better story, if it weren't for the plethora of people who've mentored and coached me along the way. The leaders whose legacies made—and continue to make—a positive impact in my life.

The best way I know to show gratitude and to honor those who've invested in me is to pass it along by investing in others.

Our influence matters. We can impact the world around us by showing up for our lives and choosing to be intentional about our legacy.

The legacy you're living. The legacy I'm living.

1. This is Bigger than Us

Who shall set a limit to the influence of a human being?
—Ralph Waldo Emerson

"Write your obituary."

The teacher looked out over our class, the elongated pause settling like the somber assignment she just gave us. I don't know how many high school sophomores stop to reflect on the obituary that will be written at the end of their lives, but I think most of us felt like the assignment landed toward pointless on the spectrum of what's-important-to-think-about-at-this-stage-of-your-life. For many of us, deciding what to wear that morning presented mind-blowing social engineering skills, leaving little mental capacity to ponder how we wanted to be remembered . . . beyond looking cool and fitting in.

And yet, Mrs. Manning possessed the uncanny ability to get her students to engage in topics outside the realm of ordinary adolescent angst and drama. She didn't just teach English, she caused us to think—and question—on a soulful level.

"And as you write, rather than simply listing the accomplishments you will have achieved in your life, think more about what kind of person you were. What difference will you have made in people's lives because of how you interacted with them? What legacy do you want to leave behind?"

I don't remember what I wrote for my obituary, but I do remember I experienced a subtle shift in my worldview. Although I didn't know all the psychological terms back then, thinking about my obituary gave me a thirty thousand foot glimpse of my life—and I knew at the end I didn't want it to be a list of checked boxes. *Surely,* I thought, *life can be lived as a grand adventure... bigger than me. Surely, there's some romantic, whimsical, fulfilling purpose out there...*

In hindsight, I can see how moments like these emboldened an already growing restlessness in me. Despite repetitive instructions on what boxes needed to be checked to be successful, I longed to break out of a system that, to me, felt broken. *What legacy did I want to leave behind?*

Amid literary terms like metaphor, allegory, rhythm, and red herring, Mrs. Manning helped us grow in emotional fluency. She asked us questions that invoked us to identify with the characters in the story. By teaching us to read with empathy and compassion, she fostered courage and conviction to become difference-makers.

One particular day stands out above the others. Mrs. Manning had just finished roll call when she looked up from behind her desk, wide-eyed.

"Oh! I forgot, I need to get a message to the Vice Principal." She looked around the classroom. "Drew, will you please take this note down to Mr. Reed for me? You'll find him in the teacher's lounge."

She handed a folded-up piece of paper to Drew and he walked out the door. Then she picked up the book we were reading, *To Kill A Mockingbird*, the 1960s classic about a black man wrongly accused of rape, a community experiencing a crisis of conscience, and the man's defense lawyer, Atticus Finch.

"Please turn to page 232." Class resumed.

But then an interesting thing happened. Several minutes later, the door opened and the Vice Principal walked in with Drew.

"Mrs. Manning? I'm sorry to interrupt your class, but I saw Drew walking down the hall. He says you gave him a message to give me," he held up the folded piece of paper, "is that true?"

All eyes turned to Mrs. Manning who stood there, befuddled, like she didn't understand what Mr. Reed just said. She glanced at Drew and then back at Mr. Reed and shrugged.

"I don't know anything about a note or a message. And I don't know why he was walking the halls instead of being here in class."

The room was silent. I didn't know about anyone else, but my mind swirled. *What? Of course she knows. We all heard her ask him to take the message for her. Why doesn't anyone speak up? What's going on? Maybe I should say something. But, wait, what do I know? Maybe I missed something.*

Mrs. Manning looked at the class before turning back to the Vice Principal and shrugging again.

Taking Drew's arm, he walked toward the door, "Alright, I'll take him down to the office and we'll deal with this." And then they walked out.

I couldn't believe it. Mrs. Manning was known for her integrity. She held a reputation of inspiring her students to live and work with a spirit of excellence, empathy, and authenticity. Everything about the unfolding scenario was incongruent with her character and reputation. And yet, no one spoke up.

"Well, where were we? Oh yes, we're on the conversation between Jem and Scout. Jem was just telling Scout how he believes there are four kinds of people in the world." She began reading out loud.

Mrs. Manning's voice was her usual calm, engaging voice. But I couldn't focus on the words. *Didn't she blatantly lie just moments ago, setting Drew up to receive a consequence for something he didn't do?* I tried to be inconspicuous as I glanced around the room.

"Naw, Jem, I think there's just one kind of folks. Folks." Mrs. Manning stopped reading. She looked up at the class and asked us what we thought about Jem's perspective and Scout's perspective. Nobody raised their hand, an unusual case for our class, normally full of lively discussion.

Minutes ticked by as I pictured Drew sitting in the office. In trouble. Because of a lie. And because no one stood up for him. Because *I* didn't speak up.

Someone knocked on the classroom door, slowly pushing it open. It was Mr. Reed again. He opened the door wider and gestured as Drew walked in, taking his seat.

"Thank you, Mr. Reed," Mrs. Manning smiled as they nodded to each other. He left, closing the door behind him.

"Can anyone tell me what just happened?" Nobody spoke. "Did I or didn't I send Drew to give Mr. Reed a message for me?"

Several heads nodded. A low murmur of agreement rippled through the room.

Mrs. Manning walked between the front rows of desks, stopping as she rested her fingertips on a stack of notebooks. "Why didn't you speak up?" She waited, meeting several pairs of eyes. "I wanted to see if we had an Atticus Finch in the class. Someone who would be a voice for justice."

The live illustration stuck with me. For a while, I was riddled with shame, *what's wrong with me? Why didn't I stand up for what was right? How come I didn't defend Drew?* I learned a valuable lesson that day. I wanted to be a voice for those who need a voice. But, I also remember the sickening feeling of not saying anything because I didn't have the confidence to be the only one to speak up.

I began questioning my beliefs and what I saw as important. Mercilessly bullied throughout my early childhood education, I longed to fit in, to be accepted. Yet, now I wondered if acceptance was worth it at someone else's expense. The world felt incongruent, and I struggled to find alignment.

What legacy do you want to leave behind? . . . A grand adventure . . . whimsical, fulfilling purpose . . .

Experiences like the one in Mrs. Manning's class that day and writing my own obituary jarred me from the ordinary, compelling me to think on a deeper, more heart-centered level. And wonder.

Life gives us clues to discover our purpose, if we'll only pay attention.

In every great story, something hangs in the balance. I knew I wanted to live a great story—a purposeful story. I didn't realize then, that purpose entails conviction. And conviction entails risk.

In the culture I grew up in, the word conviction was used in conjunction with sin. But for me, conviction was a pull *toward* something. Something bigger than me. Something more meaningful and ultimately far more fulfilling than going through life checking boxes.

Nothing made sense. Everyone seemed to be moving through one big machine with set checklists. Graduate high school. Go to college. Marry a husband who will work a steady job for forty years. Have babies. Raise them to repeat the process. It was the same in the religious institutions.

The successful people were the ones who wore the brand names, played sports, and excelled in academics. That counted me out on all three accounts. Panic and anxiety roiled in my spirit as I became more and more convinced that I was either going to be a major societal failure or I'd somehow find a way to thrive *outside* of the neat, tidy box.

And then there was that nagging conviction growing inside me, pulling me away from checklists, toward something … I didn't have a vocabulary for at the time.

There was a boy named Eric in our school who attended the classroom labeled special needs. I remember he smiled all the time, at nothing in particular. He just walked down the hallways, smiling and saying hi to everyone. And I remember his laugh was brusque and a bit boisterous—which turned out to be contagious. Everyone loved Eric. I think because Eric loved everyone.

In my mind, Eric didn't have a worry in the world. I didn't think he ever argued with his parents or did things to get acceptance. He exuded authenticity. And joy.

I started piecing together a list of the character qualities I thought might be important to live a meaningful narrative. Like Mrs. Manning said, "Think about the person you were." I knew there had to be more than conforming to the expectation of the nice girl who checked all the right boxes. The girl who conformed to fit in . . . even at someone else's expense.

There's this truth: our obituaries are written before we're dead. And you and I are responsible for deciding what story we want to live, the impact we want to make, and the vision we're going to lead. We leave legacies of resentment or love, indifference or empathy, survival or vision. We all leave a legacy.

The goal is to *live* a legacy—now—on *purpose.*

A legacy of sacrifice, conviction, courage. Love.

Legacies like the fictional character, Atticus Finch, who defended justice. Eric, whose joy splashed onto those around him. Like the teachers educating the next generation in the African Bush. (And teachers everywhere for that matter.) When you woke up this morning, you were handed a blank canvas. Well, blank except for the text across the top, which reads, "Today's legacy in 86,400 seconds."

Today matters. Your art, your message, your work matters ... You and I are made to influence hope, freedom, and joy in the people around us.

Here's what I know now that I didn't understand then: living our best version of ourselves requires risk. It requires courage to follow our conviction toward a better story.

I didn't realize that standing up for something and being a leader could feel scary and lonely. And that sometimes I'd doubt my voice, because, after all, who am *I* to speak up? And, I didn't realize these thoughts and feelings are universal. That everyone struggles with feeling vulnerable and not-quite-enough.

Yet, at my core, the nagging conviction that there's more to living a legacy than checking boxes within what feels safe and comfortable—and acceptable ... it remained. That we're *meant* to outlive our lives. I didn't know how or what it would mean. And I didn't know how far out of my comfort zone it would stretch me. Andy Warhol, a painter and filmmaker in the 1960s, is quoted as saying, "In the future, everyone will be world-famous for fifteen minutes."

A friend of mine asked me the other day if I've experienced my fifteen minutes of fame. And, you know, after considering it, I thought *why only fifteen minutes?* I'm sticking with my conviction that our lives can outlive us. In fact, perhaps the best way to honor this short time we have here on this blue sphere, is to approach each day with an influencer's mindset, *I'm going to change the world for the better. To take responsibility for the impact my life has on those around me.*

I don't know who is in your sphere of influence. But I guarantee, you have impact. You're living your legacy right now.

It's taken a long, long time and many seasons fraught with learning to forgive myself and be gentle with the process, but I'm learning that life is a beautiful mess. It's restorative. Redemptive.

Imagine the Movie How You Want It to Go

"My dream is to one day . . ." Those six words frequent the beginning of my sentences. It's as natural as breathing for me to "play the movie out in my head."

One of those dreams played out like this:

I dream that one day my child will grow up and be the kind of person who loves fearlessly. That he will be on his way to meet with dignitaries of nations when he comes across the beggar on the sidewalk. He'll stop to acknowledge him, meet his eyes, speak affirmation, and honor him with a sandwich and cold bottle of water from the nearby café. And he'll whisper under his breath, *teach me.*

A little further on, he'll see a friend whom he hasn't seen in a long time. He'll stop to ask, *What's on your mind?* Listening, inspired by his sense of wonder, knowing he has something to learn from every conversation.

As he carries on, he'll walk by a street musician. Perhaps the musician is playing the saxophone or sliding his bow across strings, the soulful strains echoing against brick buildings. He'll stop to take it all in, drop a few coins into the open instrument case, and breath deeply of the wordless discourse.

I envision it going on this way, my child alive with wonder and curiosity. Confident in who he is and aware of his contribution to the world. He takes full ownership of the plotline, looking for ways to serve, his vision full of possibilities.

At last he reaches the large boardroom where important decisions lie in the balance. He'll suspend his judgments while staying true to principles as he leans in, full of hope and wholehearted expectation.

It goes for my daughter, too. The vision is irrespective of gender. And I dream it will play out in each of my children in alignment with their unique temperament, gifts, and strengths. I picture the scene playing out in the sports arena, in medicine, the arts, in a classroom, or perhaps in a laboratory. The possibilities are limitless.

Every Scene Counts

The legacy I'd one day leave would be the one I lived in the present.

Will the movie play out exactly like I envision? Ha. I'm sure every writer would love to nail the manuscript the first time around. I'm sure the movie director would love it if every time the camera rolled, the scene played out perfect on the first take. Yet, I'm learning to live into the messy beautiful, wild, whimsy of it all.

What would it mean if we all decided to take full ownership of our legacy? If we decided not to settle? If we decided to act on the stirrings in our spirit for adventure and growth? If we followed our conviction to take a stand for others who may not have a voice, and to coach those within our influence to use their voice for something bigger, more fulfilling?

We're called to muster our courage and be faithful narrators of a different story. One in which we acknowledge broken systems, stop checking boxes, and write our lives as masterpieces.

Edit and revise the manuscript. Collect the outtakes. We'll laugh (or cry) over those later. But by all means, don't quit. The world needs your part of the story. And mine.

This is the stuff that keeps me awake at night and gets me out of bed in the morning. This living on purpose. Investing in others by narrating a story brimming with hope and vision, knowing my showing up can instill hope and vision in others.

It's Your Turn

Of course, this is all awesome in theory. Once we play the movie out in our minds, how do we go about directing—designing—the scenes of our lives?

Author, speaker, and leadership guru, John Maxwell, says, "Everything rises and falls on leadership." If that's true (and I believe it is), then imagine the transformation in our communities, workplaces, and personal lives if we took ownership of our influence. What if we cultivated cultures defined by empathy, honor, respect . . . where, instead of conformity, we expected people to bring solutions, authenticity, and conviction?

I'm going to make a bold declaration, which I believe to be true to the core of my being: You are a leader.

You have leadership capabilities and at some point, you are required to lead. Maybe for ten minutes, maybe for ten years.

In some capacity, some of the time, it is inevitable that you'll be called to step up and lead. Whether you're a parent, teacher, sibling, counselor, manager, colleague, employee, president, child, advisor, coach . . . a person whose heart is beating.

Perhaps you might be thinking, *wait a minute. What about the idiom, too many chefs in the kitchen? We can't all be directors. After all, we're not all born leaders.*

I disagree. True, we can't all direct at the *same time*. But I am obsessed with this concept of living our legacy in the present. Of rising to the occasion with courage and conviction and investing our legacy into making a difference wherever we are. First, it always means leading *ourselves* with excellence—of being the Chief Executive Officer of our own lives. And then, it almost always means bringing our influence to the moment.

This is where individuals and organizations get tripped up. Because we have a wrong view of leadership, or because we haven't invested in developing leadership competencies in ourselves or in those around us, we're prone to make decisions based on our experiences instead of timeless principles. Too often, we leave what I call relational shrapnel, in our wake. Or, we compromise our integrity. More concerned about conforming to the expectation around us, getting approval, looking good, or staying where it's comfortable, predictable, and secure, we don't step up with courage and conviction when we might make a difference for good. What if justice, healing, freedom, love, mercy, authenticity, and courage compelled us to lead the way? What if, by showing up, we embolden those around us to love more fearlessly, too?

Let's make some quick definitions of some of the terms that will show up throughout this book:

Leader and *Influencer* are interchangeable. Leaders influence. They serve. They look for ways to invest in and build up those they influence. They take extreme ownership when it comes to responsibility and look for ways to give away the credit. In our family, we built a culture around the idea that if you're leading, you're serving. And, real leaders develop the leadership in others.

Legacy and *Story* are also interchangeable. They're both something we can make intentional. They're both being written and lived in the moment.

The word, legacy, is derived from the Latin *legacie*. In the fourteenth century, it described a group of people deployed on a mission. The Medieval Latin, *legatus*, meant someone delegated for a purpose. An ambassador, diplomat, agent, messenger. How amazing is it that you and I are here for such a time as this, ambassadors and agents of honor. Men and women of valor.

Deployed on mission, delegated for the purpose of living more wholehearted stories, creating solutions, and envisioning possibilities.

And I can't get over how uncanny it is that the word legacy looks like legend. The Medieval Latin version, *legenda*, means things to be read. What if we all show up for our lives with the mission to be legendary in the way we love, honor, and serve those around us? What if we greet each day acknowledging that our lives will one day be read? What if we consider, *what do I want to be known for?* What if, in light of eternity, we purpose to not squander our time, but to live all in? How might our impact be read if our narratives resonated with authenticity, integrity, and conviction?

> *"I've learned that people will forget what you said, people will forget what you did, but people will never forget how you made them feel."*
> —Maya Angelou

As we're scripting the story we want our lives to tell, it's essential to be aware of the influence and impact we have on others. *What difference will you have made in people's lives because of how you interacted with them?*

After mulling this over and experimenting extensively in my own life in the places I lead, I've decided leadership is four-dimensional. At any given moment, we're living in one of these dimensions of leadership. Let me explain.

Four-Dimensional Leadership

Lead Yourself

First, there's self-leadership. This is the equivalent to applying the oxygen mask to yourself before you can help those around you apply their own oxygen masks. It's in the foreground because you need to invest in yourself to have something to give. It means investing time, money, and energy in self-development through a vast array of tools: books, podcasts, conferences. It means seeking out and investing in coaches, counselors, and mentors to guide you through learning curves and processes. It means investing time reflecting and what author and neuroscientist, Dr. Caroline Leaf, calls *thinking about our thinking*.

This is the part in our story where we consider what we want written in our obituary. It's where we consider which character traits we're going to internalize to live a purposeful, impactful legacy. Self-leadership is deciding what's most important to us—and making our lives a reflection of our principles and values.

I've experienced whole seasons in which I got swept up in a mad life current, not able to make a clear purpose statement, let alone envision what I wanted. I know these seasons are part of life, but let them be just that, a season. While there's no set length of time for a season, whether it's an hour, a week, or many months, the mindset that it's a season, keeps the perspective that *something* will eventually change. Inertia doesn't last forever. (I'll share a story about this later.)

Personally, I finally learned to give myself extra grace during difficult seasons. I learned to be kind to myself.

Take good care of yourself so that you come out the other side charged and ready to go.

Take care of yourself throughout the day:

- Stretch. In fact, right now, as you're reading this, tilt your head to one side for a few seconds and then the other side for a few seconds.
- Breathe. The kind where your breath extends your stomach, hold for a couple of seconds and then exhale to the count of ten. Do this two or three times. If I'm laying down, this is the breathing that puts me to sleep.
- Drink plenty of water. I drink a glass of water first thing in the morning. I also keep a thirty-two ounce water bottle with me at all times. My goal used to be sixty-four ounces of water a day, but since becoming a habit, I usually end up drinking much more than my self-imposed minimum.
- Talk to yourself. Seriously. Our subconscious believes whatever we tell it. This isn't a secret. If we're going to change the story of our lives, we need to reprogram the hardware in our brains. Whatever untruths we believed in the past need to be rewired with truths. Our thoughts program our mindsets and our mindsets determine our actions. And our actions produce results. We must take responsibility for the thoughts we think.

- Take a power nap. I can't figure out why naps are underrated. A ten- to twenty-minute rest acts as a turbo boost for my day. (My family teases that I can fall asleep anywhere, under any condition, and they're right. But, sometimes, even a two- to five-minute span of closing my eyes and letting myself drift off, can be just what I need to catch a second wind.)
- Intentionally develop daily habits. One of the most crucial differences between those who consistently achieve their goals and keep their commitments and those who don't, are the success habits high-achievers build into their day. Consistent, healthy, daily habits are the oxygen that ignite confidence, motivation, and passion—all emotions that wane unless fueled by *action*.
- One of these habits is a morning routine. One of my heroes, author Claire Diaz-Ortiz, changed my life with one of her axioms, "By leading your morning, you lead your life" (*Greater Expectations*, 2013, 37). I know it's eight simple words, but I'd tried for years to develop a solid morning routine, all to no avail. Until I heard her use that axiom. It resonated and acted as the trigger that finally helped me hone a routine that energizes me and stokes my vision for the day ahead.

Another success habit, (albeit, this is weekly with a daily application which I'll explain in a moment), is to set aside twenty minutes with some paper or a couple of pads of sticky notes and a pencil. There are different ways to do this, but I've learned that the key is to keep it simple.

Set a timer for ten minutes and on the paper or sticky notes, write down everything that brings you joy in life. The stuff that makes your heart beat fast with excitement and anticipation. This isn't the time to edit yourself. If you're using sticky notes, jot one idea per note.

When you come to the end of your ten minutes, read through your list and find three you'd like to complete in the next thirty days. File the rest away.

Next, write three action steps for each goal that will get you closer to achieving that goal.

The idea here is to do everything fast. I promise that tomorrow when you wake up and come to the sudden realization that there's an important step missing in between steps two and three on one of your goals, you can edit. That's the point. This whole beautiful mess is meant to be lived forward, with momentum. It's taken a long time, but I'm learning the beauty and power of writing the story forward, editing, and changing course.

Put this paper (or sticky notes) where you'll see it every single day. This is the mistake I made for years. Putting my goals and aspirations on paper comes easy for me. But then I'd file them away and not see them again for six months or a year. I finally realized that keeping them front and center, keeps them top of mind. It's a lot easier to work toward something when I know the end goal.

Now, here's the daily application of coming up with those three goals. Every evening before going to sleep, look over your three, and for each one, write down an action to take the next day that will move the lever closer to achieving that objective. It doesn't matter how small the action might seem, if it moves things forward then that's what counts. It's not how many minutes or hours we have in a day, it's what we do with the time that matters.

Once a month, set aside a minimum of a couple of hours to reflect and write a list of things you'd like to do in your life. Every ninety days, schedule a mini-retreat with several hours to reflect, and yes, once or twice a year, schedule an extended multi-day retreat for the same.

These are only a handful of examples of self-leadership . . . some of the most basic. But our strength of character—our integrity—is foundational to our ability to lead from a heart of love and service. Exercises like these help solidify who you are, who you're becoming, and what to invest in as you live a purposeful, impactful legacy.

These habits will not only cultivate excellence in your own life, but they ripple throughout your team. As leaders, we have a responsibility to be the leaders we want our people to be. When they see you invest in self-development, self-care, and activities that support the mission and vision of the organization, they're inspired to follow suit.

I learned through trial and error that habits form our character and character forms who we are. When emotions took precedence and a lack of motivation set in in our home, we reminded one another of our axiom, "I care more about your character than I do your happiness." It's a way to uphold a standard that communicates: habits lead to character, character leads to discipline, discipline leads to freedom, and freedom leads to living a fulfilling, impactful legacy.

Lead Those Behind You

Next, adjust the setting on the lens slightly, and those who aren't far behind you come into focus. In this case, your leadership bears authority or expertise. It's the dimension of leadership most people think of when they consider the word 'leader.' You might be the manager, the parent, or perhaps the fifth grader mentoring the third grader in his reading. With the intent to cultivate a leadership culture, I've told our children since they were young, "You're a leader. That means you look for ways to serve and honor others."

It's easy to give to others when we've been poured into. Our stories are replete with those who are ahead of us and find joy in reaching out for our hand to help us to the next step. It's a privilege to turn around and do the same for those who want to emulate our success in who we've become or what we've achieved.

Lead Your Peers

Switch your lens to wide-angle and you'll see the next dimension of leadership, those within the group. Those on the journey alongside you. This is where leadership might not be so obvious, but it's no less crucial.

I found a fantastic example of this kind of leadership while reading the book, *Switch* (2016), by authors Jake Knapp, John Zeratsky, and Braden Kowitz from Google Ventures.

Jake and his partners explain how they go into businesses and solve big problems in one week. By putting a strategic team of peers together in which everybody brings their unique insight and expertise to the project, they're able to go from a big problem and no answers on Monday to a solution and prototype to test on Friday.

Another place I see this dimension of leadership is within military teams. At first, all the members on the team are trained in the same basics, but then each person on the team masters a specific skill so they're more effective on missions. I love this concept and see it as invaluable to run more effective and productive teams in every setting from boardrooms to family rooms, from politics to surgical theaters.

Lead Those in Authority Over You

The fourth dimension of leadership is situated higher and a little further in the background. It's the leadership dimension to which I get the most baffled responses when I teach this to individuals or groups. So, I'm on a mission to debunk the myth that it's not possible to lead those in authority over us. Not only is it possible, it's imperative. And a wise leader will allow themselves to be led by a subordinate on occasion.

I can think of two examples . . . one which saved lives and one which has simply enhanced life and made it more fun. The first example comes from a book I read a while back. In *The Mission, the Men, and Me* (2008), author and former Delta Force Commander, Pete Blaber tells the story of a mission he commanded in the Middle East. In the early morning hours before dawn, the men positioned the tanks and readied themselves for battle.

"Watching and waiting behind our guns, we could hear our breath as it froze in front of our faces.

"In an instant, the ghostly city roared to life. Enemy muzzle flashes blinked across the urban horizon like flashbulbs at the Super Bowl, except these flashes shot tracers" (2008, 2). Enemy fire and their positioning revealed they needed to abort the mission and pull out of the firefight.

In the midst of the chaos and noise, the men on the ground (take note of those last five words) were radioing for instructions. And this is where the story takes an interesting turn. Pete saw his men in trouble, but just as he ordered his men to pull back, the general in command over *him*, ordered Pete to tell the men to proceed into the city.

Outnumbered, in a precarious position, and with the enemy drawing closer every minute, Pete had to decide. With his job at stake, he made the call. "Pull back to the desert as ordered," Pete said over the radio (2008, 11). Because of Pete's decision, no lives were lost.

Where was the general located during the firefight? "From his temperature-controlled operations center, the commanding general saw the battle as a series of color-coded computer icons on a giant flat-screen television." During "intermittent satellite radio transmissions," Pete described the unfolding scene to the general. Yet, the "commanding general had no context" (2008, 8-9).

It was the men on the ground, experiencing the brutal reality of the mission, who provided context. This is important, and I'll cover this more in a later chapter, but we need leaders at the top who are humble and will listen long enough to gather context from "the men on the ground" before charging forward.

From the time my children were babies, I've maintained that they are my gurus in many areas. Aware that there are times when they have "on the ground" insight, it's part of my job as a leader to listen for relevant feedback and either make decisions accordingly or (as they grew in maturity) support them in their decisions. There were times when I didn't yield, didn't listen, and carried on with a foolhardy decision, regretting it in the end. I've learned the wisdom in listening to those who might see something I missed. Besides making parenting more fun, listening for context has deepened the trust and bond in our relationships.

Beyond the Fabled Fifteen Minutes of Fame

How might the scenario in Mrs. Manning's real life illustration played out differently if even *one* of us demonstrated conviction over conformity? If any one of us demonstrated courage and spoke truth to power? You know, it's interesting, despite what I perceived as a trusting, open culture in Mrs. Manning's class, no one took a stand for what was right. Perhaps from time to time, there needs to be an honest evaluation of whether the people in a culture feel they're surrounded by people who have their back. There's something to be said for too many directors, but it's a tragedy when *no one* leads the cause.

Questions starting with "How might I..." or "How might we..." signal my brain to go from passivity to activity. They help me think in terms of possibilities and experimentation. With love as my guiding principle, I play the future "movie" in my mind. It's crucial to believe that you have impact. That you can make a difference. That you not only have more in you, but you are capable of helping others develop their full potential, too. We can change our own internal script ... And we can change the scripts in our workplaces, communities, marriages, and everywhere we have influence.

I received a huge compliment the other day from my daughter, Israel. She said, "Mom, you're so likeable." As I let her affirmation sink into my soul, she added, "I think it's because you like everybody ... your expectation is that people are likeable." It's true. I do expect people to be likeable. This world is full of brilliance. How amazing is it that us humans have this immense privilege to interact, share ideas, create stories together, and live legacies abundant in rich, meaningful relationships?

But I didn't always have that expectation. I went through seasons in my past in which *I* was the toxic person who was difficult to get along with. This is why I'm adamant that people can change . . . Safe people with healthy boundaries believed I had more in me than the toxic attitudes and behaviors I displayed.

By gently, consistently calling out the greatness in me, friends, mentors, and coaches helped me rewrite the scripts I told myself, so that I could live a better narrative. A *different* narrative. They helped me edit out the cynicism so that I could instead live a legacy of love.

Our words hold the power of life and death. By telling ourselves a different story—a new script, we change our expectations. When we change our expectations, our emotions will align with where the story is going.

When I type text on the computer, and then delete, the words are gone. I type new words in their place. I know this is all obvious, but I see this as miraculous. Powerful. Life changing.

Passionate.

Epic.

How might we change the world—one person, boardroom, business, family, at a time—if we not only lived brave into our purpose here on earth, but we confidently interacted with those around us, believing we can help others live better narratives, too?

It's exhilarating to help people find their voice. To live forward into coaching, mentoring—leading—others. To show others how to be wholehearted, spurred on by a purpose that'll outlive them. I'm eternally grateful for the mentorship of people like my English teacher, Mrs. Manning, and the joyful example of Eric.

I'm thankful for the privilege to be able to say, "My dream is to one day . . ." confident I can lead with vision and that it doesn't have to be perfect because I can edit and revise along the way. And I'm thankful that I don't have to cram a legacy into "fifteen minutes of fame." That I can live it in the present, mindful of the seeds planted for future fruit.

Equipped with insights and strategies, we're imbued with confidence and courage as we set out to author a new story. I know this. I've lived it. This book and my entire philosophy behind the value of leadership and coaching is a result of my own life experience.

As I mentioned earlier, throughout my early childhood years, I endured bullying. Socially awkward, low self-esteem, and a "daydreamer" whose grades consistently ranged from low "C" to "F," I found solace in books. Our home was filled with non-fiction with most of them in the leadership and self-help genres. I became fascinated with mindsets and human potential and the ability to overcome setbacks and obstacles. To transcend circumstances.

Stories of inspiring people who served, loved, forgave, and helped others . . . people whose legacies inspired greatness and purpose in others, filled my time when I wasn't in school. Turns out, they were my leaders. My coaches. The ones who encouraged me to raise the bar and think long term.

I don't claim a system that says "well hey, it worked for me, so it'll work for you." I just know that I've read too many stories and known too many people personally who changed their narrative, not to believe it's possible for anyone.

We can all get to that place where we feel like the best we can do is survive and endure. That place where we don't realize our significance, settling instead for "the best that one can hope for." But I'm telling you (and you can imagine me leaning forward over my steaming cup of tea, eyes wide and intense), life on this planet is really, really short. A blip on the radar of eternity. We're made for *more* than settling.

We can regain sight of the vision—and help those around us do the same. We can learn to craft a story so compelling that we transform the script—and then teach others to craft a compelling story, too. I know because I've had many mentors, counselors, and coaches throughout my life who've come alongside me and prompted me to make my life a masterpiece.

I found those coaches in the books I read, in real life, at conferences, and online in their blogs, webinars, and courses. Like those children in the African Bush who did whatever it took to be at school to learn, and the teachers who showed up day after day, passing the torch regardless of limited resources, I am privileged to have had access to so many masters whose legacies planted seeds in my life. Coaches and mentors whose legacies became legendary as their stories impacted those around them.

What impact might your legacy have on someone today? In being a man or woman of valor, how might you be legendary in the way you show up for your life and love in a big way?

2. CRAFTING YOUR LEGACY

Risk more than others think is safe.
Care more than others think is wise.
Dream more than others think is practical.
Expect more than others think is possible.
—Cadet Maxim, U.S. Military Academy

Do Work That Matters is the mantra of the new Millennium. While it has a nice ring to it, what, exactly, does it mean? How do we know if we're "doing work that matters?"

I typed "productivity" into my Internet search engine and it showed 215 million results. Over 40 million results appeared when I typed in "productivity apps." In the pursuit for ways to get more done in less time with improved quality, society has devoted entire areas of science into the research of productivity. *Hustle* and *automation* are modern buzzwords.

Yet, even as the frenetic speed of achieving more increases, us humans still crave meaningful interactions and relationships. Things we can't hustle or automate.

So, how do we ensure we're not just showing up, going through the motions, punching a time clock, and checking boxes?

This book, the book you hold in your hands, is the culmination of a twenty-two-year experiment. An experiment that lacks multimillion-dollar funding, laboratories with the latest technology, or data and statistics. Well, I guess there's data—my own personal data collected through personal experience—but, for all intents and purposes, the data has been written into the narrative.

It's an ongoing experiment that asks the question, *What is the story we want to live through our personal and professional lives?*

Jim Loehr writes in his book, *The Power of Story*, "As its very name suggests, a movie's primary intention is to *move* the audience emotionally. Story is the vehicle through which the movement occurs. Story is what stirs us, terrifies us, breaks our heart. A boring story fails because it doesn't move us, doesn't tap our capacity for empathy. Think of the very best stories you've ever seen or read or heard, and you remember the depth of your feeling for one or more of the characters" (2007, 55).

People sometimes say to me, "Oh, you're a writer. I could never write. I'm not creative." And my response is, *your life is telling a story.* Is it filled with purpose? Vision? Passion? Is it compelling, adventurous, whimsical?

The Way It Works Here

As a new parent, the work ahead of me meant developing our story, figuring out what we'd be the best at, casting vision, all the same systems and ideas it takes to build a team of champions in any setting. Both my husband and I had aspects of our stories that we wanted to implement, while there were others we knew we didn't want to repeat. It's like we were coming from two different corporations with all our beliefs and experiences and the nuances and idiosyncrasies of our respective corporate entities, merging via marriage, and forming a new corporate entity. While a corporate merger is quite different from the sacred covenant of marriage, there still exists expectations, both spoken and unspoken.

In each new endeavor and commitment, we need to ask the question, *what is this for?* How might we love big through this marriage, parenting, organization, community effort, business? We mustn't be haphazard. It's imperative that we get crystal clear on the vision. After listening to hundreds of leaders share their stories, I know this is a challenge every leader faces.

My husband and I would create a culture that would one day leave a legacy—either by default or intentionality. I knew I wanted it to be the latter.

The very first leadership book I ever read was *Everyone's a Coach: You Can Inspire Anyone to Be a Winner*, by Don Shula and Ken Blanchard. My mother gave it to my husband, LeRoy, the same year our oldest was born. Her inscription on the inside reads, "Christmas, 1995, to LeRoy. I trust this book will encourage your heart and help you to build others up, including Eli. May God bless you, Mom."

I read it immediately, absorbing the ideas and philosophies. *This is it,* I thought. *This is my sweet spot. I want to invest this one life here on this planet pouring into people in my sphere of influence, inspiring them to be their best version of themselves. To be champions. My husband, my children, and whomever else I meet on this adventure.*

The book inspired me to think purposefully about the legacy we wanted to live in our family. It set me on a quest to build a team of champions with a vision for service that would extend beyond the boundaries of our four walls.

It formed my Why to the work—the mission—of serving others. I wanted to help others succeed. And it caused me to want to learn everything I could about becoming a visionary leader—the way Coach Don Shula did for the Miami Dolphins and Ken Blanchard did for those he served as an executive coach.

Nineteen years later, our friend would ask our son, Isaiah, a compelling question that caused me to lean forward in my chair.

"Why are you this way?"

Our second oldest, Isaiah, finished taking another bite from a barbecued chicken leg. I thought, *Great question!*

We hadn't known this family for very long, hence their dinner invitation to deepen the friendship. Throughout dinner, the conversation volleyed between questions and stories. Now, with a small stack of empty bones on our plates, we leaned back in our seats content.

And that's when the dad commented to our children that he noticed they asked intelligent questions, kept eye contact, listened. (For the record, their children did the same.) He paused, then asked, "Why are you this way?"

Isaiah looked across the table. "What do you mean?"

The dad leaned forward and folded his hands together, looking intently at him. "I mean, tell me why you ask good questions and then engage by listening. Why do you look people in the eye when they're talking to you?" He paused. "Who taught you kids to care? Who taught you to be interested?"

Isaiah took another bite of chicken, perhaps hoping one of his siblings would answer. All four of my children glanced at one another and then at me. Finally, Isaiah shrugged his shoulders, swallowed, and said, "I don't know. I guess it's just how our family is."

I guess it's just how our _____ is. Fill in the blank: office, company, neighborhood, school, organization . . . marriage, family, faith community . . .

The teacher in the African Bush, and how he said something similar, "The way it works here . . ."

Our lives are telling a story. So are the places—the cultures—where we live out our lives. Do we know the story we're telling? Do we grasp our impact? Do we evaluate our failures and successes? Do we know why we are the way we are?

That conversation sparked a soul search and caused me to take a step back. To ask myself the questions that have inspired entire books and topics of research.

Jim Collins, author of *Good to Great,* quotes one of his favorite professors from Stanford Business School, Robert Burgelman: "The single biggest danger in business and life, other than outright failure, is to be successful without being resolutely clear about why you are successful in the first place" (2001, 213).

Collins' professor makes an arresting point. I realized I'd be remiss if I didn't pause to consider our successes—and our failures—and be resolutely clear about why we're "the way we are." Every marriage, family, workplace and organization has a story it's telling. In choosing to build a culture focused on making an impact on the world around us, it led us to persist in personal and leadership development. Which was great, a lot of the time. And a total failure at other times. Every day, ordinary family life continues to shape and hone our character and our culture. And from that spills a story.

At the end of the day, we get to appraise. Like playing the game back in slow motion, asking ourselves and one another, "What worked? What didn't? What did we learn? What will we do differently in the culture of this family to align our story—the legacy—with our principles?"

I can do what so many have done for me: I can tell you what we did. I can tell you what worked and what didn't. But my passionate plea is that you would think through the story *you* want to tell . . . the legacy you're living in the present.

Someone's hope and inspiration may be on the other side of your decision to live your best version of you. To live bold and brave. To outlive your life by sharing the gifts inside of you. But first, it's crucial to get crystal clear about who you are and what you want. First, as individuals, then as communities.

How can we think we're "just doing life"? What if we maintained awareness that every time we speak is an opportunity to share vision? To share joy and ideas and art and romance and passion?

Why are some marriages dynamic? Why do some marriages seem to thrive, exuding joy and playfulness, achieving dreams and goals, while others seem to stagnate, going through the day-to-day routines with a more or less ambivalent attitude?

Why are some homes filled with grace and peace while others are filled with tension and angst? Why are some families filled with a sense of adventure while others are bored but lack the desire to change?

Why do some parents have joyful, nurturing relationships with their young children and healthy, fun relationships with their adult children?

Why do some companies attract some of the most creative and productive people? How does a company get on the list of top ten companies to work for?

Why do some brands have an enduring and inspiring message while others fizzle over time?

Jim Collins published *Good to Great* in 2001. Although I added it to my "Must Read List" when it came out, I only recently read it this past year, fifteen years *after* it was published. Because of this, I had to console myself with patient, gracious self-talk as I devoured timeless principles and brilliant concepts which would have helped me immensely fifteen years ago.

At one point while reading the book, I had an animated conversation with my children about "getting the right people on the bus." Collins asserts, "... if you have the right people on the bus, the problem of how to motivate and manage people largely goes away. The right people don't need to be tightly managed or fired up; they will be self-motivated by the inner drive to produce the best results and to be part of creating something great." He continues, "... if you have the wrong people, it doesn't matter whether you discover the right direction; you still won't have a great company. Great vision without great people is irrelevant" (2001, 42).

After reading this aloud, I looked into four pairs of contemplative eyes, waiting. After a moment, my seventeen-year-old, Ezekiel, said, "Mom, it's easy. You just have to raise your kids to be the right people on the bus."

Easy, my son says.

There's only about a thousand factors to consider. I smiled.

And this is where the cliché rubber meets the road. This is where intention and thought enter the story we're writing.

As leaders, we can either hire self-motivated people with the inner drive to produce the best results and to be part of creating something great, or, *create a culture from the ground up,* where we *develop* people to live from a place of abundance. To live from a place of *I am enough. I have resources to be helpful and there's more on the way.*

My high school English teachers inadvertently taught me leadership principle number one: Show, don't tell.

Master myself. Live a compelling vision that inspires people "to be part of creating something great."

Later, when it came to raising a family, leading an organization, and facilitating workshops and small groups, I sought to learn and model the same disciplines I expected from those within my influence.

We can be the visionary leaders we want to see in the world.

Who are we? and *Why?* and *What is this for?* are mantras at the forefront of this ongoing experiment. Together, my husband and I are raising up four members of the next generation. That's not a stewardship we take lightly. And so, it is with passion and vision and a sense of mission that we press on, not only for those living within our four walls, but for every family on the planet, as well as those in the corporate world whose enduring cultures makes for an inspiring and impacting legacy.

"A great organization is one that delivers superior performance and makes a distinctive impact over a long period of time" (*Good to Great and the Social Sectors*, 2005, 5).

Given the ages of my children, I have about a twenty-two-year tenure in this training and consultancy firm that we call family. A twenty-two-year window of opportunity to invest in bringing out the best in those I serve. To rigorously and deliberately study their strengths and interests. To champion and challenge them toward excellence.

We want our story to be one of character and eternal values. Of pursuits in which relationships and connections with others are our highest priority. Of servant-leadership and developing people who are driven by transcendent goals and aspirations.

Great, you may be thinking. *It's too late for my family, the office where I work, the business I run. We're years into this process. I didn't build a foundation based on principles, vision, or values. We're surviving and I don't know how to get to thriving.*

It's not too late to start where you are.

Develop Your Storyboard

Children's authors, novelists, movie writers, and playwrights use a tool called a storyboard. In blocks of eight, with a total of twenty-four, thirty-two, or forty as a typical amount, the author fills in the squares with the text and illustrations. The entire story is laid out on one page, giving the author a visual of how the story will work from page to page.

It's a great idea to do this with our lives from time to time.

Similar to an action plan for businesses, a storyboard shows us the ebb and flow of our lives. How one season slowly unfurls into a collection of wonderful memories, while another season might have us looking for the horizon as we hold desperately to a shred of hope. It's a way to realistically look at where we are in the present and determine what we need to revise to move us toward our vision.

Thinking about our lives in storyboard form helps us see that the plotline is simply that—the plot. The circumstances do not define us, but they do help inform our decisions. It took me a long time to realize and embrace that truth.

A storyboard gives us a visual of where we're headed. It enables us to move toward the vision, evaluating the milestones along the way so we can course correct, edit, and revise.

Lifestyle design is a relatively new term. Yet, I realize this is how I've thought all along. The meaning is how it sounds, designing the life you envision living. It's the opposite of checking boxes and conforming to a set of assumptions. It means challenging the status quo and writing a storyboard authentic to the purpose for which you are created. In marketing, there is a simple formula businesses use to describe their purpose. "_____ is the only _____, that _____, for _____." Fill in the blanks with the *name* of your company, *what* you do, *how* you do it, and *who* it's for.

Domino's Pizza is a classic case study: "Dominos is the only restaurant, that guarantees hot pizza delivered in thirty minutes or less, for college students."

Here is an example of our "organization's" (aka, family's), purpose: The Olson's are the only family, that leverages leadership principles and entrepreneurial mindsets to strategically develop leaders for world class teams.

(Side note ... I just now made that up. And it took some monumental brainstorming, an hour of procrastination, and the devouring of chocolate and peanut butter. Yes, I made it up based on our *actual* mission statement, but to write it in a concise, poignant way that communicates the vision is no small thing. I'm with you.)

Now it's your turn. What is your institution's *Mission: Impossible*? What are your audacious goals? What is your purpose? Why are you the way you are? Does everyone know *the way it works here*? Does everyone know the legacy you're striving to build?

Several years ago, I was talking with my friend, Arlana, about the importance of the "mission." I asked her what their family "was all about."

She thought for a moment and then told me, "Faithfulness."

Then I asked her what her children would say if she asked them.

She smiled, curious. "Huh. I don't know. We've never really talked about it in such clear terms. Let's ask them."

A few minutes later, a gaggle of young people came in from the yard where they'd been running and playing games. At the time, her two were eleven and fifteen years old. After pouring lemonade in several cups, she asked her children, "What would you say is our family's mission? What is most important to us?"

Without hesitation, they both repeated their mother's word: "Faithfulness."

Arlana smiled, pleasantly surprised. Or maybe not. After all, their family *lived* faithfulness. Anyone who knew them knew faithfulness was core to their culture.

That's the thing. It's not just some nice little decorative calligraphy we stamp across our walls or paint onto a stressed wooden plaque. As cool as those things make our homes and businesses look, what matters is the integration of those ideals into who we are to live meaningful stories. Stories that *impact.*

The pastor in our faith community asks from time to time, "If we ceased to exist, what would the community lose?" By asking this question, he challenges us to stay on mission.

What about you? Your marriage? Family? Workplace?

There's More to the Story—Challenge the Status Quo

We lived just a little over two miles from the high school, only a (slow) 40-minute walk from our house. Every time I walked to school or back home, I passed the juvenile detention center, located almost exactly between the two.

And I wondered.

I wondered about the kids locked up in rooms. Or were they behind bars? What had they done to end up there? What was the staff like? Were they kind and patient and helpful? Were they ill-tempered and cynical? What did the delinquents (or were they inmates?) think about the fact that they were in detention? Were they remorseful or calloused? Bitter?

And I couldn't stop wondering about the story they dreamed for their life when they were younger. Surely, no one dreams of growing older and getting locked up.

Two things happened as a result of my curiosity. First, I decided I'd go tell those kids that they could write a better story. A more meaningful story. One that stretched beyond themselves and found fulfillment in loving others. That I just knew that they were created with a destiny—a destiny that did not include jail.

So, one day, I marched up the front steps and rang the bell. Someone from inside pushed a button, causing the simultaneous loud *bszzzzz* and the click of the door as it unlocked.

"Can I help you?" A man got up from his desk and walked to the counter.

"Yes, I'm here to volunteer." I couldn't tell for sure, but I thought I detected amusement in his eyes.

"How old are you?"

I didn't see what that had to do with anything, but I obliged. "Fifteen."

"I see." He pulled at his chin with his thumb and forefinger. "Well, here's what you need to do. You need to finish high school and then go to college and get a degree. Sometimes people volunteer as a college internship. Then when you finish, we can hire you."

The second thing that happened is that every time I walked past that detention center after that, I whispered to myself, *that can't be it. I know there's more to this story.*

What could I do? I hoped that somebody on the inside was telling my peers that they didn't have to write the story the way it was being written—that they could write it different. I knew some pretty great adults. Maybe a few worked on the inside, helping them write a more meaningful narrative. I'd love to tell you that I found a way to encourage my peers. That I got involved in the school leadership council or some other group that made a positive impact.

Unfortunately, I too, eventually chose not to take responsibility for the narrative I wanted to write. Although I didn't land in juvenile detention, I succumbed to settling for the status quo. *Just graduate high school*, became my only goal. It was a goal that seemed to satisfy the adults in my life, still provide plenty of time for me to hang out with friends, and hike the foothills of the Rocky Mountains.

Many years later, I experienced another *There's more to this story* moment. I was eight months pregnant and at the end of a year of checking boxes at the community college. With zero career aspirations (back then, the world didn't consider traveling the world and writing about it a viable career), and dreams of being a mom, I decided to figure out what moms did. What was the job description?

Our faith community hosted a local moms group. When I learned that moms could attend during their pregnancy with their first baby, I went. After all, I thought, if you don't know what you're doing, surround yourself with others who are already doing it and learn from them.

I don't remember who the speaker was or what the topic was that day. I vaguely remember the small group conversation being mostly about how tired everyone was and about baby milestones like teething and weaning and moving to solids and about "terrible two" temper tantrums.

I remember moving into "craft time," and there, in the middle of constructing an origami frog greeting card, tears welled up in my eyes. Excusing myself from the table, I hid in the bathroom and tried to pull myself together. I set my hands around my unborn son and whispered over him, "I believe this is far bigger than nappies and pacifiers and the latest designs for bouncy seats." I paused and breathed deep.

I dried my tears and went back to the table, where I gathered my jacket and the almost-finished origami greeting card and made my way to my car. As I drove home, romantic notions of how I pictured motherhood collided with my judgments of my perceived reality: the tired, frumpy, frustrated moms I had just met.

From what I had just experienced, I knew that I wouldn't find fulfillment in making crafts. At least not in the "crafty" sense.

I wondered why the conversation about milestones and terrible two temper tantrums evoked such a distressed reaction in me. And if I knew what I didn't want, fine, what *did* I want? Overwhelmed with anxiety, I feared losing control. I longed for our family to live on purpose . . . joyful, whimsical, adventurous . . . to influence and lead with impact, vision, and passion. Would I have to give all that up, consumed instead with . . . the ordinary? I knew what it felt like to settle for status quo and this time . . . *this time* I wanted it to be different. There wasn't a man on the other side of a tall counter telling me I needed a degree to positively influence and impact the humans in my care.

Panicked, I tried to console myself with an internal rant, *surely, parenthood exceeded every other type of work on the planet in terms of importance. People went to fancy universities, wrote theses* and dissertations, and accumulated letters after their names to do the work I was about to embark on. Developing the potential in the people I lead—specifically my children . . . was there anything more important? With more eternal significance?

Gracious. *Now* I know that those aspirations are universal to us moms. Of course, what did I know that day I attended the moms group? I hadn't even birthed my first baby!

Now I know the reason I didn't hear about their deeper aspirations is because they were simply in a safe place where they could be honest about their utter and complete *exhaustion*. A level of emotional and physical exhaustion I couldn't possibly empathize with until I experienced motherhood myself. (I've heard reports that entrepreneurs of startups, doctors in residency, and soldiers in combat experience similar levels of exhaustion.)

Until I found myself in the thick of the journey, I couldn't grasp the concept of living passionately, gracefully, whimsically in the beautiful mess. Imperfect. Exhausted. Needing to lament to another mom about severe sleep deprivation. And learning to embrace extraordinary in the ordinary.

Still, I reaffirmed out loud to my unborn baby as I pulled into the parking space in front of our one-bedroom apartment, "You have a destiny. And in a couple of years, you'll be a *Terrific* Two."

Yes, later, in the middle of those occasional all-out tantrums, I had to repeat the mantra, *Terrific* Two. Led by my conviction that as leaders, it's our mission to call out the greatness and potential in those we impact, I stuck shamelessly to my idealistic view: while temper tantrums are terrible (and exhausting), *people* have potential to be terrific. And, honestly, despite trying to convince myself, I didn't always *feel* the truth of my mantra. This is why it's important to value our emotions without being ruled by them.

Believing there's more to the story than what is seen, takes *faith*. It's believing and calling into existence that which is not, but we believe is on its way.

Affirmations and declarations determine the course of our lives. The stories we tell ourselves are the ones we live from and the mission that drives us.

In hindsight, I would have spoken more grace and forgiveness and aspiration over me, too. How many days, tired, frumpy, frustrated filled in the spaces on my storyboard. *Now*, I'd tell my younger self, *it's okay. You're enough. Embrace imperfectly perfect.*

As a leader in the workplace, are you careful about the words you use to fill in your storyline? Do you speak potential and destiny over those you lead? Are you gracious and kind to yourself on those days you struggle?

As someone thrust into the role of people development, I wanted our milestones to be character qualities—habits of excellence—set within a culture of grace. I set out to create a culture in our home based on the stark reality that our time here on Earth is short—a brief blip on the screen of eternity—and we can design a storyboard rich with impact and intimacy.

We're called to live in this tension between the now and the forever, an eternal perspective in which we must remain fully present in the moment. It's a sacred space, yet raucous with life. It simultaneously requires a sober mind and child-like faith. Careful thought and joyful spontaneity.

To write our stories beyond ourselves, with greater meaning, freedom, and fulfillment. To become the best versions of ourselves so that we can help those we lead, do the same.

To be professionals in the business of life.

I listened to an interview the other day. The successful businessman being interviewed said that he and his colleagues had just finished a two-hour "vision" meeting.

I thought, *What if we made that kind of investment into envisioning what we want our marriage and parenting ventures to look like? Our businesses and organizations? The narratives we're living in the places we inhabit?*

This idea of seeing people live fully into freedom—purposeful, passionate, pouring into and helping others build authentic, wholehearted legacies—why don't we have a "vision" meeting for our lives?

"Why are you this way?" our neighbor asked my children, and I am asking you now.

Why are we this way?

What is the story on our storyboards? Do they need editing? Revising? Are they true to our purpose? Do they call out the greatness in us, so that we'll more naturally call out the greatness—the *Terrific*—in others, even in the midst of a tantrum? How might we love big through the culture of our corporation, our community, our congregation, our team? Our *lives*?

3. Identity Leads the Storyline

God made man because He loves stories.
—Elie Wiesel, Holocaust survivor, author

The only thing that walks back from the tomb with the mourners and refuses to be buried is the character of a man. This is true. What a man is survives him. It can never be buried.
—J. R. Miller

Wired for Story

I knew I wanted to create a culture that honors individual uniqueness. To architect such a culture, it made sense not to focus on performance but to honor personhood. What we do is essentially an extension of who we *are*.

"I've learned to hire based on attitude." The comment came from my dentist friend who owns his own practice. "I learned the hard way, that we can teach nearly anyone the skills and competency to do the work," he paused as though reflecting on past scenarios, "but there's no way to correct a bad attitude. And one bad attitude is all it takes to make an entire environment toxic."

I hear it over and over again. Entrepreneurs, CEO's, managers ... story after story of the person who didn't have the character necessary to move the team and their goals forward. More and more companies are hiring based first on character qualities and then on job qualifications.

Here's what I learned from the leaders in my life . . . attitudes are products of a belief system. And our beliefs are formed out of our experiences. But sometimes we don't tell ourselves true stories about those experiences and in the process, we limit our potential.

Chris LoCurto and Joel Fortner are helping business leaders and entrepreneurs take their personal lives and companies to the next level by helping them get clear on their vision. Through one-on-one intensive coaching, masterminds, and live events they help clients break through mindsets that are holding them back. LoCurto's and Fortner's life purpose is helping individuals and businesses "realize and maximize their personal and professional potential."

On a recent call with Joel, I was amazed by the depth and level of engagement and passion he infused into the conversation. What I assumed would be a simple informational call turned out to be a powerful, encouraging, and transformative connection.

They're skilled at helping people identify where they are, where they want to go, the actions to take to get there, and how to remove the obstacles standing between them and their goals. With expertise in personality styles and communication, they're invested in working to help leaders discover overlooked opportunities, gain clarity, and increase their revenue.

Once their clients gain a clear perspective, they're able to exceed previous limits, achieving a return on investment in hard metrics like revenue but also in their personal happiness, growth, and relationships.

We're not damned to stay stuck in limiting belief systems. We're not victims to mindsets that hold us back.

I heard a story once about an entrepreneur who had built up his business only to make some choices that caused him to lose it all. This happened twice.

Discouraged, and facing the task of starting over, he shared his story with a mentor who had achieved success in his business both in revenue as well as in impact in the world.

After listening, the businessman encouraged him by telling him how great it was that he had failed twice. He went on to say that he didn't work with anyone who hadn't ever failed in business and then reiterated the affirmation that it was even better to fail twice.

We all fail. It's how we choose to respond and how we apply the lessons we learned along the way, that will determine our personal growth and the direction we want the story to go next that matters most. Chris LoCurto and Joel Fortner help their clients achieve massive breakthroughs and go to the next level in every area of their lives by helping them identify and play to their strengths.

I imagine my phone call with Joel was a glimpse into the energy and passion and growth their clients experience through the expert coaching they receive. Their mission is to develop leaders who make an impact from a place of courage, conviction, and confidence in who they are as a person.

And it's not too late to start where you are.

During a leadership conference, I heard a CEO tell the audience that they intentionally don't hire anyone for upper-level leadership if they haven't made at least a six-figure financial mistake at another company first. His comment jolted my senses as I leaned toward the edge of my seat. He told the audience their company asks questions to get the person to relate the story from his or her view. What his company really wants to know is, do they blame shift or do they take ownership of failures? Are they able to learn from failure? Do they take the lessons and apply grit and resilience to future goals?

It got me thinking about the culture in our home. My husband and I both come from strong backgrounds of people-pleasing and self-worth based on performance. Failure meant our personhood was somehow innately flawed. Pain-avoidance, risk-aversion, fear, shame, and control became tactics we employed to validate our worthiness. I knew that to build a culture in which our narrative was authentic and wholehearted, we'd need to assess our current reality and live from a different place. A different storyboard.

We needed to tell a different story about identity—and delving into the topic of identity has changed everything.

Your Mindset is Key

"At conception, you were a person of dignity." The woman on stage paused to let us absorb her words. I was attending yet another leadership conference and though I don't recall the speaker, I remember her words and how my thoughts reeled with objection, *before I had a chance to prove myself?* Yet, somewhere inside of me, I allowed the audacity of that truth to begin to heal the broken, shame-riddled places.

I reasoned, *If I'm a person of dignity, then it makes sense to live a dignified life. In fact, it's my* responsibility *to live into and create a culture of dignity—a culture of honor—wherever I have influence.*

This epiphany became the defining theme of the narrative I wanted to tell.

Unearth the Extraordinary Potential In You

My grandmother read to me at bedtime whenever I stayed the night at her house. She opened one of the faded, worn *Uncle Arthur's Bedtime Stories* books, chose a story and asked me the same question every time. "How tired are you? Do you want me to read slow and monotone or would you rather I read animated?" I gave her my preference, pulled the crisp white sheets up under my chin, and entered scenes of children my age.

From Donald, I learned the value of keeping my promises. Martha demonstrated the value of trying again after failure. And there was Gerald, who learned the hard way about the Golden Rule, his daddy patiently and wisely guiding the lesson via Gerald's indulgence in the gooseberries. The power of forgiveness came alive in the story of Jackie and his toy yacht. And I listened intently as my grandmother read about Georgie, who went from selfishness to— you guessed it—helping others.

During the day, I curled up in one of the old recliners with two stacks of magazines nearby: *Reader's Digest* and *Guideposts*. One after the other, I read them cover-to-cover. My favorites? The "Drama in Real Life" stories in *Reader's Digest*. Story after story of real-life characters displaying courage, sacrifice, care, and concern for others.

When I wasn't listening to or reading stories, I imagined them. My world consisted of dangerous escapades in which I played the cunning detective, the bounty hunter, a resolute ninja who fought for the underdog, or an undercover princess who fought for justice.

At some point every school year, my teachers arranged a private conference with my parents to confront the issue of my wasting time in class with daydreaming. Every meeting ended with my earnest promise to try harder to pay attention, to stop daydreaming . . . but to no avail. For as long as I can remember, I've imagined who I wanted to be.

Here's the deal, if we woke up with oxygen in our lungs and a beat in our heart, we can be what we wanted to be. We can take one step, no matter how small, toward our goals. As we mature, we learn it's not so much about taking on specific roles as it is about integrating the character qualities of someone who stands for justice, loves big, brings a sense of playfulness and joy, and calls out the greatness in others. Yes, maybe we'll one day be a surgeon, a photographer, a recording artist, or a parent. But, titles don't describe our identity or character.

Maybe instead of asking our young people what they want to be when they grow up, we need to ask them what *kind* of person they want to be. *Who* they want to be. Maybe we need to change our question to reflect that what this world is really looking for is people who live from a sense of dignity, worthiness, love, freedom, and abounding hope. What if we coached our young people to think about what it might look like to contribute to the world from a place of inspiration, wonder, and curiosity?

I'm still enraptured by story. More than ever, I'm fixated on the idea that we can learn from failures—in fact, *leverage* the lesson to *propel* ourselves forward. We can choose a champion's attitude, live from a place of dignity, and practice the habits of real life superheroes: patience, wisdom, forgiveness, compassion, generosity. Resilience, grit, tenacity, and courage.

And here's what I'm learning about paying attention: Cognitive studies show we think in story, sorting raw data and organizing it in such a way as to make sense of the relationships and circumstances and our place in the unfolding plot. We humans want to know what comes next. We draw inferences, stack our experiences, and come to conclusions. Our brains don't like randomness so we search for context, for patterns.

Many years ago, I shared with my friend and mentor about the anxiety attacks I was experiencing. When I finished describing the utter and complete feeling of overwhelm that descended, she said, "Sharon, here's what you're going to practice: Put four raisins on an otherwise empty table. Then, one at a time, you're going to focus on a raisin. Think about its' texture and size. Then, as you chew the raisin, count ten breaths slowly and concentrate on your breathing."

At first, it sounded hokey, but I followed her advice. And an interesting thing happened. Although I only did the "raisin exercise" once, I started to slow down, observe, be present throughout the day. My conversations became richer. I listened better. And slowly, I became more attuned to the thoughts and feelings of others. I learned to empathize. Over time, I trained myself to *stay* present . . . to breathe. To consider the context of the moment, listen to my heart, to consider the layers of the plotline.

Well, I'd like to say "trained" as if the lesson is past tense. As if I've mastered the art and science of staying present. But this morning proves I'm still in process. While thick in the revision process of writing this book, I resorted to all the classic procrastination tactics. I took an extra long nap, spent an hour watching social media videos, cleaned my office, read a book, ate, cleaned the kitchen, and made a snack before finally turning to the most important task of the day.

A replay of the morning demonstrates my propensity to succumb to old tapes playing in the recesses of my subconscious. Paralyzed by fear, distractions are a welcome reprieve. Unearthing our full potential feels risky.

Honestly, it's in these vulnerable moments when I revisit the story my life is telling, the story I *want* to tell, and *who I am* in this story. I battle the invasion of old mindsets, *I'm not disciplined enough, smart enough, patient enough . . .*

These are the moments of truth. Or, rather, *un*truth. To think about our thinking and our belief system. The moments when we have the privilege—and ultimate responsibility—to choose a storyline which reflects the truth. The truth that we're created with dignity. A people of valor.

The Latin word for dignity is *dignitas*. It means "worthiness." To lean into that truth, embracing the concept of our worthiness as our identity, well, it's no small thing. To simply show up—and keep showing up—even after running away, failing, or dropping the ball altogether. To say, *wow, I'm afraid. But I'm going to press into purpose and trust the process.* It's in these moments when the air feels scarce and our chest is tight, that we must force ourselves to breathe the oxygen of *I am enough*.

One day, at the end of a writer's critique meeting during which a group of four of us shared excerpts from our manuscripts in progress, my friend, Sarah, put her hands on my shoulders and looked intently at me. "You are enough."

She said it matter-of-fact, like it was the most obvious truth in the world. A knot formed in my throat as I choked back tears. Blindsided by my reaction, I wondered, how did three little words evoke such a torrent of emotion?

I smiled and turned toward the table, "I'll help you clear these dishes." Thankful for the diversion of something as tangible as a few plates and wine glasses to take to the sink, I busied myself in hopes she wouldn't say anymore. She didn't. But I've played those words over in my mind ever since.

How might it change the way we live our lives, run our organizations, and love those closest to us if we lived from a place of dignity, honor—worthiness? From a place of *enough*? How do we live *that* story?

How might we transform our relationships if we speak hope and potential into those we lead?

We are created with all the potential to construct an epic narrative. When I was in junior high, *Choose Your Own Adventure* books were popular. They were books in which the reader, a few pages in, was presented with two different paths, "If you decide to walk down the alleyway, turn to page 17. If you decide to enter through the front door of the mansion, turn to page 23." Once I started a book, I'd exhaust every possible outcome before I'd put it down.

Curled up on the couch, I'd arrive at an ending and I'd think one of two things, *What a stupid ending. I'm going back and trying the other option.* Then I'd go back and choose page 23 instead. Usually, it had a better resolution. I'd smile satisfied, *Okay, good ending.* Even if my first choice turned out satisfactory, I'd wonder, what if I'd agreed to explore the library inside the mansion instead of getting lost in a maze of alleys?

Throughout my life, I battled depression and anxiety. *Perform, perform, perform* was my mantra. *Don't disappoint. Keep your head out of the clouds. Pay attention,* I'd remind myself. Whatever role I found myself in, I scrambled to find *Three keys to being the perfect wife, The ten areas in which a parent mustn't fail, How to be the ideal friend.* In the process, I forgot the basic fact that stories are created from process. There is no one-size-fits-all. Maturity requires you and me to humbly integrate knowledge and vulnerability within the context of our unique story. Every moment is a chance to make a decision that's congruent with who we *want* to be. To embrace the beautiful mess in the process.

What? You mean there isn't a hard and fast formula to ensure I get it perfect? No wonder I wallowed in anxiety.

Beliefs Lead the Storyline

In the book by Dr. Henry Cloud, *Integrity: The Courage to Meet the Demands of Reality,* (2006), he asserts that telling ourselves stories about the way things are is one thing; after all, we're wired to make sense of our world through the stories we're telling ourselves. But whether we have the character to tell ourselves *true* stories is what makes all the difference.

For years, I compared my marriage to other marriages. I read marriage books, attended marriage retreats, and sought advice from friends whose marriages appeared to have what I was looking for: two imperfect people somehow creating a (fantastical) perfect union. Then I'd apply the information in an effort to make our marriage the "way a marriage is supposed to be." When it didn't work the way I envisioned, I felt disappointed. Why did it work so well for them? What was I doing wrong?

One friend in particular has a marriage that's vivacious, fun, adventurous, intimate … *sizzling*. A model marriage, from my perspective as well as many others. So, I went to the wife for marriage advice. And then I tried to integrate her advice into our marriage. But I only ended up frustrating my husband and myself. Finally, one day I realized that I had completely ignored the fact that every couple has their own marriage personality. Every family, organization, and entire corporate structures have their own personality. Their own *cultures*. Those who are successful are the ones who wisely glean truths, principles, and insights and integrate them into the storyboard of their unique culture.

It's extraordinary to be in a world in which we can derive inspiration and wisdom from brilliant sources all around us. It's a gift to learn from others—to be the proverbial fly on the wall. As long as we avoid comparisonitis, and stay true to our principles and purpose.

I'm learning to take a lifetime of experiences and insights and synthesize them into the unique storyboard that makes up the culture in our marriage, our parenting, and our community. Things change. People change. To accommodate growth and needs and perspectives requires intentionally listening to and noticing the stories happening around me. To stay in context. Notice hope. I can raise my standards in congruence with what I'm learning and who I'm becoming. Insight upon insight, every decision can change the trajectory of my story, create impact, enlarge my vision, and build a legacy of contribution. Those childhood bedtime stories? They're not daydreams anymore. For any of us.

Every moment we're still here offers us the gift of living from a place of dignity that says, *I am enough. I contribute my unique greatness. There's more resources on the way. I will look for the clues that life offers, fight for the underdog, and contribute to something bigger than me. I'll search for patterns and context, then integrate them into who I am to narrate a new story.*

In *Pour Your Heart Into It: How Starbucks Built a Company One Cup at a Time*, (1999) Howard Schultz describes how he gleaned insight into an entirely different culture surrounding coffee. At the time, the owners of Starbucks sent Schultz, an early employee, to Italy to find prospective roasts to import to their store in Seattle. But during his visit, Schultz discovered something besides Italian roasts. As he meandered through the city, he found people sipping espresso while engaged in conversation. Day after day, he passed the same espresso stands and saw the same customers taking their afternoon breaks, connecting with one another. People lingered in a culture that values community and relationships. And it set him to wondering: what if Starbucks built a culture where coffee is simply a means of creating an environment that helps people connect?

Schultz could have stuck to the simple task of obtaining Italian roast imports. Instead, he noticed people. He observed the cultural nuances. He imagined how he could integrate the new information. As a result, he revolutionized the culture of Starbucks.

Schultz helped Starbucks change their story from an errand, "stop by Starbucks and pick up a bag of coffee," into a worldwide movement, which sells coffee and tea to foster connection between people. Like the *Choose Your Own Adventure* books, Schultz essentially changed the storyline. He stayed open, looked for context, and thus, his vision enlarged.

We're not obliged to follow a broken, archaic, or stagnant system. Schultz didn't. Instead he wondered about new possibilities. We can all become what I call Possibilitarians—people who live from a hope-filled place of endless possibility. We can remember who we are—people of dignity and worthiness, who have ideas and dreams, and make an impact. We can break out of the status quo.

Growth. Sacrifice. Commitment. Empathy. These are the declarations—the mindsets—we can choose to write into the storyboard of our lives. They become the defining principles and therefore the vision from which we'll live.

Who are you? Why are you the way you are? What is your *vision* for the person you are becoming and for the story you want to tell? What compels you to raise your standards and live a story bigger than yourself based on character, conviction, and courage?

Our answers to those questions—who we believe we are, and why—will determine the value and impact we bring to the culture around us.

Yesterday I was removed from a volunteer position on a planning committee. For the last few months, I was difficult to reach, missed mandatory meetings, and didn't reply to messages in a timely manner. After several merciful attempts to engage my help, the leader sent me a message, graciously letting me know that I was relieved of my commitment.

My heart fell. At first, I felt guilty that I had let the team down, causing extra time and effort on their part as they tried to reach out to me. Then, about an hour later as I processed the larger implications of my irresponsibility and carelessness, I succumbed to deep discouragement.

Questions like *Will I ever learn to be responsible?* and *Why do I sabotage relationships?* played through my mind. Thoughts infiltrated my mind: *I can't be counted on. I have nothing to contribute. I'll never change.* I didn't speak them aloud, but my heart heard the messages clearly. The chatter inside my head was toxic, full of self-condemnation and self-pity.

My son, Isaiah, put his arm around my shoulders, speaking encouragement more powerful than my emotional wreckage: "Mom, the same thing happened to me several months ago. I committed to change, and I did. It's okay. Everyone experiences things like this. You need to decide what you want to be known for and then live into that."

What you want to be known for . . . who you are . . . and then live into that.

How does a person who takes ownership, handle failure? (Because, *that* person? That's who I *want* to be.)

This place of vulnerability . . . phew! it's uncomfortable. Last night, we went around the table, doing what we do during almost every family dinner. We answered the question, "Tell a story from your day." (Well, I guess that's a statement. But we have mostly men in this house and I've learned how to "ask questions" so as to provoke answers beyond yes and no.)

When I shared the story of losing my place on the planning committee, they offered empathy and grace. They patiently listened as I took full responsibility, explaining my lack of communication and commitment. They didn't excuse my behavior or minimize my wrong. Nor did they judge or condemn.

And there's the crux.

Brené Brown asks in her book *Daring Greatly* (2012, 217), "Am I the adult that I want my child to grow up to be?"

Not only that, am I the influence that I want those in my organization to be? I'll say it again, *we can be the leaders we want to see in the world. We lead by example.*

I had failed to follow through on a commitment. But I wanted my children to know that a failure doesn't have to become our identity. These moments are crucial. In the face of failure, we can either succumb to the deception that we are a failure—that our personhood is innately flawed—or we'll believe the truth that we are a people created with dignity and potential. We can embrace the messy process.

I related to my family the rest of the story about how I resolved the situation by taking ownership of my irresponsible decisions. I shared the conversation I had with the coordinator later in the day and about her gracious response. How that she didn't "let me off the hook" but simply offered forgiveness.

Do those in my sphere of influence witness times of failure in my life and see me handle it with humility and grace? Do they see me engage in the discomfort, both with myself and anyone else with whom I need to make amends? Do they see me take ownership?

I may not have lost six figures in revenue for our company, but failures of any magnitude measure our character, resiliency, and grit. They reveal whether or not we'll take ownership and if we'll leverage the failure for personal growth.

I really do want to change. I don't want to be known for lack of follow-through and commitment. But I'm a little braver today than I was yesterday. It's a powerful thing to be surrounded by the kind of energetic, positive, encouraging people who expect levels of excellence from me.

Not perfection. Excellence.

So, this culture, the story we're telling through the culture of this family—is this the storyboard we envisioned?

Moments like last night affirm the path we're on. I'd love to tell you that every mistake, every wrong, is handled with so much empathy and grace. But we are, after all, human. We've been known to shame and speak insult over injury. And we've witnessed the emotional fallout in the team morale.

Herein lies an important point: We'll always follow the storyline being told. And at any point, *someone* can step in and change the direction.

This is why it's one of our core values to develop the leader within our people (in our case, our children). Everyone on the team needs to know they have a responsibility to stay true to our culture's values—and that one of our top values is creating a safe place for people to take risks, experiment, and fail. We're striving to build a culture of action-takers and learn-it-all's living outside of our comfort zones in an environment where we extend grace without accepting excuses.

So what happens when shame creeps into our culture?

Just the other day, my husband and I had one of those ugly moments in which he made a mistake and I played the I-told-you-so card. Ezekiel, our seventeen-year-old, overheard as he walked through the room. He came back, leaned over to my ear, and whispered, "Grace." Then he winked at me and walked out.

Ah, yes.

There's an example of what it looks like to take note of the trajectory of the story, to be someone who steps in and . . . edits. *Remember,* this *is who we are. This is who* you *are. Live from this place.* We all have greatness to bring to the world around us. Sometimes, greatness calls us to be editors—to be the one who says, *Wait, time out. Based on the vision of where we want this story to go, the present script isn't matching up.* Those Choose Your Own Adventure books? They gave me a sense of empowerment. *Hey, I don't like how that option turned out. Let's try different strategies more aligned with who we are and who we are becoming.*

Having a vision for who we are becoming is crucial because it will lead to what we stand for.

The other day, my fifteen-year old struggled through a difficult circumstance, but instead of facing it with a champion's attitude, she resorted to being argumentative, disdainful, and negative. (*She gave me permission to share this story.)

Realizing the emotions were too high to reason with her, I reminded her I wanted to hear everything she wanted to say, provided she was respectful. I moved onto the same couch with her and turned directly to her to let her know she had my full attention.

And then she shared her rant. My posture communicated, *your heart is safe with me. You are enough and nothing will change that.* I remained with her without getting entangled in her emotions. Several minutes later, she sat there quiet, waiting for me to respond. I moved a little closer and said, "Look in my eyes and tell me what you see."

"Eyeballs." She crossed her arms across her chest and squinted her eyes.

"No, tell me what you see reflected in my pupils."

"A nucleus?" The sass in her voice and the hint of a smile at the corners of her mouth told me we might be on the verge of a breakthrough.

"Do you see your reflection? Because the young woman you see reflected in my eyes is bold and daring and loves people deeply.

She's kind and thoughtful and has faith to move mountains." Her jaw unclenched and the expression in her eyes softened. "That's who you see. Now, live from *that* place."

It didn't mean circumstances went her way. But what it did mean, is that it brought her back to her identity and from that, she can determine the course of the narrative.

Of course, you're not going to get this intimate with an employee or colleague. But the principle is that our words hold the power of life and death and we have a responsibility to raise the expectation and speak destiny into the lives of those we hold accountable.

Sometimes, we need to set the example for others by speaking life over ourselves so they can see what it looks like for themselves. This happened at an event I attended a couple of weeks ago.

I walked in early, so there were only a few people already there getting the registration and refreshment tables ready. As I walked in, one of the gentlemen turned to me and said, "Shame on you! You didn't fill out the online registration form correctly and I had to go in and fix it for you."

Taken back momentarily, I asked him to clarify the situation for me. He did and then reiterated, "I'm shaming you. You caught that didn't you?"

I apologized and thanked him for fixing the problem for me, asking for further instructions on what to do next time. He gave me instructions and then once again asked, "You know I shamed you?"

Smiling, I responded, "Yes, I heard you. But I don't receive shame. When we make a mistake, we need to remember that our failures don't define us. Next time, I'll do it the correct way and ask you if I have any questions." I don't know how he took that, but my sincere hope is that he understood he doesn't need to take on shame, either.

Our brains are the most impressive storage centers ever created. From as early as in utero, our brain begins collecting memories which are imprinted in our subconscious. Every sight, sound, smell, touch, and taste gets written into the archives of our memory. As we grow older, these imprints define our perceptions. Our perceptions create our belief system about our identity which translates into our behaviors.

As we learn and grow and mature, we need to be cognizant of whether our perceptions are serving us or acting as obstacles to fulfilling our full potential. Like when we write a new computer program over the top of an old program, we need to reprogram our minds in the areas that don't help us reach our potential. Through counseling, coaching, and accountability we can get help to re-story the storyline.

In the past, I would have received shame spoken over me because I used to think shame was my identity. But I've since learned that failures and mistakes don't define me. Failure is something that *happens*, it's not who we are.

To identify our core values, we may need to re-story our story.

Re-Story as Necessary

My friend, Mary DeMuth, is a powerful example of taking a narrative filled with childhood sexual trauma, victimization, shame, abandonment, and rejection and claiming victory on all fronts instead. As the author of over thirty books as well as a popular conference and retreat speaker, she is a storyteller who is on a passionate mission to bring restoration, healing, and hope to those whose stories are filled with pain and hopelessness.

She quotes Carl Bard on her website, "Though no one can go back and make a brand-new start, anyone can start from now and make a brand-new ending." Through her own Re-story events, she is a compassionate, gifted teacher who helps her audiences envision a new story.

In the process, they realize the truth of their identity as someone created with dignity and worthy of love. From a place of emotional freedom, they're able to write a *new* ending filled with healing and hope.

There are far too many people living from a place of shame and fear. I'll talk more about the benefits of accountability in chapter five and growth and healing in chapter seven, but for now, let me reiterate, we're designed to live from a place of freedom. When hope doesn't frame our stories, we're prone to resort to self-preserving behaviors to survive. When we don't understand our unique contribution to the world, we're apt to settle into complacency.

The option is to seek help and get healing. To re-story our lives. Because once we get a clear vision of what *can be*, we become unstoppable. By changing our mindset, the possibilities become limitless and we'll be able to identify our cause, our purpose, our unique reason to endure. And knowing why we do what we do, what we stand for, and the reason for our guiding values, we'll move toward our true north.

In his book *How the Mighty Fall*, Jim Collins asks, "What would be lost if we disappear? What is our reason to endure? Successful people never compromise on their core values. What do we stand for?" (2009)

Who are we? And what do we stand for? What does that *look* like in our culture?

The answers to those questions make all the difference. Look, it revolutionized a tea and coffee store into an entire culture where cups of deliciousness foster connections.

Get Crystal Clear on the Vision

One evening after the children were tucked in bed, LeRoy and I sat at the dining room table talking. We were out of debt and he was finishing up his degree in Social Work. We were enjoying the quiet and decided to take advantage of no interruptions by having a more serious conversation.

"Being that we're debt-free, we can invest money." I don't remember who brought this up out of the two of us, but it's one of the defining conversations of the culture of our family.

"Let's invest everything we have—our time, money, energy, knowledge, material possessions . . . every resource—into whatever we can take with us into eternity."

Sometimes, more so during late-night conversations such as this, it seems to me, you find yourself on "sacred ground."

Then, just for fun, facetiously, we wrote down on a piece of paper "A List of Everything We Can Take With Us After This Life."

"Well, the first one's obvious," we both said at the same time.

We smiled smugly as I wrote down: *People.*

"Okay, next one . . ."

I wrote: *Relationships.*

We looked long at each other. The smugness was gone and in its place was a profound sense of *this is going to define our story. This is who we are.*

This is the vision: *People investors.*

And all the most important questions, like *What is our family's purpose on this Earth? What are our core values? What does the world need, that our family culture is uniquely equipped to provide?* culminated in turning the trajectory of the plotline toward a lifestyle that would outlive us.

I wrote: *To add value to every single person who crosses our path.*

This became one of our family's axioms. A guiding beacon in a values-driven culture.

Since LeRoy was attending school full time, I knew that I'd need to be assertive about finding ways to invest in self-development. It made sense that I wouldn't be able to give that which I didn't have and so, along with self-development, I became passionate about learning how to develop others, making it my mission to look for the best in everyone and seek out ways to help people become the best versions of themselves.

Oh, but it's a journey! All great adventures involve risk, don't they? We've crashed and burned too many times to recount. We've summited a few proverbial mountains and slogged through some miserable valleys. And then there's the astronomical baggage fees—figuratively speaking—as we've lugged around lack. It's ironic how much lack weighs. Especially lack of confidence.

Learning to live from a place of identity where *grace* and *love* trump *performance* is a lifetime journey. It requires humility. It challenges us to step into vulnerability, to be transparent, and to reach out to others for accountability. It's a terrible and beautiful thing to experience those moments in which our beliefs are jarred and our assumptions challenged. And the jarring of beliefs and challenging of assumptions happens when we take action toward our goals. When we make a decision, *I'm going to go down this road*, and we take one tiny step toward our goals. When we execute.

To grow, to mature, to stretch . . . the journey is worth it.

One of the first lessons I learned about entrepreneurship, running a successful company, and leadership is that the most difficult person to lead is me.

But with the advent of that late-night conversation, we knew the vision was to develop the people in our "corporation." With an audacious vision for the story we wanted to tell through the culture of our family, we needed to figure out which values would drive that vision forward.

These were the values attributed to character qualities that LeRoy and I needed to zero in on with laser-like focus. And if growing in character to lead with integrity meant embracing vulnerability, then grace would be our spotlight.

Leadership is a bold adventure. It requires the courage to take a long, honest look in the mirror before setting out to build a legacy. The bottom line: the intricacy and intimacy of the relationships along the way is too big of a trust to set about without a clear vision of our own identity.

As leaders, we must ask ourselves what we want the results to be. What do we want to be known for? Not *our* renown. We want those we lead to understand that we *see them*, value their personhood, and desire to bring out their best.

And they're all we get to take with us.

So to move toward the vision, develop the culture, and live the story of our unique "brand,"—to envision our storyboard—we need a way to make decisions consistent with who we are.

We need to know our core values.

4. The Power of a Tenacious Vocabulary

*Life is not a journey to the grave with the intention of
arriving safely in a pretty and well-preserved body.
But rather, to skid in broadside, thoroughly used up,
totally worn out, and loudly proclaiming,
'Wow! What a ride!'*
—Anonymous

"Remember who you are. Be a good leader."

Our children grew up hearing those words. They were spoken every time they left our presence.

Grace-based.

Character-driven.

A culture of honor.

My husband and I had to invest time and thought into the vocabulary we wanted to use to tell our story.

Through reading stacks of books, talking to mentors and coaches, and listening to the language used in business, I collected lists of words. And I persisted in asking questions.

How is it that you and your parents have such a close relationship?

How did you build a bond with your children?

How did you create a culture in which your volunteers show up consistently and cheerfully?

How did you learn the kind of leadership in which you bring out the best in your people?

Who taught you to be a great communicator?

Who are your mentors?

How do you play to your strengths and how do you figure out other people's strengths?

When have you failed, what did you learn, and how did you get back up and keep going?

I relentlessly asked questions and hung on every word as people shared their stories. And through those stories, I learned. (And still do.)

After a couple of years, I sat down to construct a framework for our family's "storyboard." And honestly? It was intense. Unfortunately, I naturally kept defaulting to performance-oriented vocabulary. I had to write on sticky notes: *Who are you? Who are you becoming?* to remind myself to stay focused on the dignity of personhood. We envisioned a story of service to others that developed from the values that defined our culture.

We wanted performance, ambition, aspiration, goals, and achievements to be the *tools* to build character and the *results* of uncompromising principles and a core set of values.

As of this writing, we've been on this journey for twenty-two years. In hindsight, I can see places where we detoured. Times when we settled for "good enough." (Which I've since learned is not only okay, but a healthy, imperfectly perfect view in some instances. Brain surgery, not so much. Setting out on your next travel adventure, good enough works.) Whole seasons in which we threw up our hands in fatigue and discouragement. I can also see countless times when grace superseded our failures. When our faith community surrounded us with support, challenged us to press on, led us, and believed we had more in us than we recognized in ourselves.

This last week, I gathered around a table with other women. In the entrance of Katie's home, their family values hang on the wall. I stopped to read them and thought, *Like my friend, Arlana, if these weren't printed and hung where everyone can easily see them, their values would still be known. This family's culture of service and love-centered, faith-filled leadership is evident because their lifestyle exemplifies their values.*

Do those you lead and impact honor the culture they represent? Do they take ownership of the values that define your culture? How do the words you use match the vision of your organization?

How Might We Make the World a Better Place through Our Unique Corporate Culture?

The topic of culture came up in a conversation with friends over dinner the other night. We were amongst military personnel, and they were "talking shop." I leaned in, intrigued.

"You have all these young recruits coming in who aren't from homes that taught them values. They don't come from a culture of self-respect and respect for others, strong work ethic, or ambition. We have to give them a vocabulary for ambition."

A vocabulary for ambition.

It is imperative to consistently keep the values of the organization in front of your people at all times. Know the vocabulary. Use it often. Every day. All day long. I extracted vocabulary words from a stack of corporate vision statements. Then I wove them into our culture's storyboard.

Sure, script looks great—poetic even—hanging on a wall. But make the words a part of your everyday conversations and decisions. Use the *exact* words from your storyboard in normal, ordinary instances. In so doing, you'll create a culture in which the people you lead can internalize the core values. And once people internalize those values, the values integrate into the context of your culture.

Arlana's children knew their family was about faithfulness because the word and its meaning is used in context on a constant basis. They *live* faithfulness.

I know I sound repetitive right now.

That's the point.

When our children argued, we reminded them (if we discerned we needed to intervene—but this is another topic of conversation), "You're an Olson. In this family, we value gracious, respectful conflict resolution."

Grace. Respect. Conflict resolution.

When we faced challenges, we reminded one another, "We're Olsons. We've got this. We value problem solving."

Problem solving.

When caught up in selfishness, we remind each other of our family's mission to build a culture of honor—requiring us to make decisions based on a heart's attitude of humility and servant leadership.

Honor. Humility. Servant leadership.

And when we derail, veering away from our values, and seek selfish ambitions? Our family's values point us back to our guiding principles. They point the way back home.

I intentionally slowed down, learned to breathe, considered the context of the moment, and then found ways to demonstrate what our values looked like in everyday moments. I labeled and named their identity over and over.

Not only did I remind them of our core values in the struggles, but I consistently called out their identity when their actions demonstrated our family's vision.

You choosing to give up your turn to let that stranger go first? That was selfless. You keeping your commitment when something more fun came available? You inspired me when you honored your commitment. You giving the bigger piece, (or the last piece), to your sister? That was generous.

Selfless. Honorable. Generous.

In business, they call this the feedback loop. And it's the wise leader who closes the feedback loop to stay engaged with those they influence. It communicates, I see you. And thank you for carrying our team's vision forward.

For many years, our family's mission statement sat in plain sight on the mantel or a bookshelf so that it could be referenced on a constant basis—a true beacon. Then one day, after our family already (mostly) integrated the mission, values, principles, and vision, I decided to condense the 115-word document into three words: Make Grace Tangible.

Living out our family's values, reiterating them over and over again all along the journey, gives our people a mindset. A frame of reference. Sure, we have them printed and framed, sitting on the shelf in our living room. But, more importantly, we've referenced and lived them until they've defined the culture of our family. Being in a value-driven culture has given us the vision for who we're becoming. And where we're going. And they've helped guide the story we're telling.

Sure, there's the question, *What are you willing to die for?* Though we believe the better question is, *What are you willing to live for?*

What makes your heart beat quicken? What keeps you awake at night and gets you out of bed in the morning?

One of our family's favorite questions—one, I'll admit, we need to ask more often—is, "Describe your ideal day based on the person you want to be." All ideas are put on the table. This is a fun exercise because it stirs our imaginations and gets us thinking about the plethora of possibilities. It's a heart-based practice, so answers like,

"I live on the thirty-fifth floor of a Manhattan studio apartment. Since I work from home as a writer, I get my morning coffee and start work at my desk, situated in front of floor-to-ceiling windows overlooking the city," serve as fuel for one another's big dreams.

Here's the big idea regarding the dreams of an ideal day . . . once you share it with those around you who believe in you, and support your big dreams, you give them permission to speak congruency over you. In other words, if your actions are incongruent with your stated vision, your teammates will hold you accountable. This is how it works when you're part of a team of champions. You all believe everyone on the team has an epic story to live and you call it out of each other. Grace doesn't give way to excuses. Grace calls out excellence.

In 2006, I got to be part of a team which hosted an evening once a month for women to connect and be encouraged. We designed the event to challenge the status quo and help participants be braver and more creative. Every month included stories and training meant to equip, inspire, and use words that empowered and spoke to the (sometimes hidden) hopes and vision in women.

One of the best parts of these events were the team brainstorming sessions leading up to the event. On a quest to find ideas to make the experience dynamic, we threw ridiculous concepts and notions onto the table. We explored many of them. We experimented with a few. And in the end, we'd end up designing the evening from the two or three winning ideas out of as many as fifty or more.

The *other* best part was the speakers. Every month, we'd find a woman who lived what she preached. A woman whose passion—and vocabulary for ambition—described her lifestyle. These were ordinary women who lived their art, shared their message, and loved deeply those who came into their sphere of influence.

Give those who work and live within your culture a vocabulary for ambition. And then brainstorm ways to *act* on those ambitions. Which of the ideas make sense to pursue later and which ones fit with your current season? Be sure to file the ideas that are "out there" for posterity's sake.

What are the problems in our world? How is our culture uniquely equipped to contribute solutions to help people live with greater freedom, deeper joy, and more meaning?

These are the questions we constantly ask ourselves. Questions like these keep us in a state of wonder with a service mindset.

"How might we _____?"

And then, "Do you find this question as interesting as I do? Want to join me in trying to answer it" (from the book *A More Beautiful Question* by Warren Berger [2014])?

We can, (and must), question the status quo in the cultures where we live and work. It's up to us to oversee the vocabulary. To make sure it helps those in our communities live the vision of where we're going, the story we're telling, and the values we embrace to get us there. This is the call to all leaders everywhere in every setting, be it marriage, the corporate or non-profit worlds, politics, churches, schools. Everywhere.

When it comes to the power of our words, we must not "let the chips fall wherever they may." We must be custodians of the values in our cultures . . . and give people a vocabulary that calls them to the vision of who they are and who we are as a culture.

5. A Culture of Accountability

Responsibility is the price of greatness.
—Winston Churchill

Discipline equals freedom.
—Jocko Willink

"Exercise, exercise, exercise."

The male voice blared through the bullhorns throughout the military base. For months, military personnel hustled to get their troops ready. From the top commanding officers to the newest recruits, as well as civilian personnel, everyone had one thing on their mind: the upcoming UCI (Unit Compliance Inspection).

Although its name changes, the Air Force calling it a Unit Compliance Inspection or the Army calling it the Organization Inspection Program, it always means the same thing. It is an event that calls on every person's best efforts to meet regulations.

Fascinated by the intensity, I engaged people in conversations to learn more. As a civilian, I wanted to understand why whole squadrons worked extra hours, some of them putting in twelve-hour days for four or five months, "just to get everything ready to pass an inspection." This was how I phrased my question to friends when I inquired about their long hours and focus. (Cultural dissonance doesn't just happen when in foreign countries.)

I received a glazed over, never-mind-you-wouldn't-understand expression. They changed the subject. Or, after more prodding, they gave me a vague, "Oh, it's just something we have to do every so often in the military."

So, why was everyone uptight? Why all the extra hours? Why were my friends going in on weekends? And sure, we moms and our children carried on, ignoring the voice coming through the loud speakers whenever an exercise was announced. But it meant something else to those who were practicing for the coming inspection.

My husband tried to explain: "Every 't' must be crossed and 'i' dotted. Three-ring binders with regulations and official forms must be updated and in order. Then those need to be perfectly organized, easily accessible. Floors and walls must be scrubbed, door jams dusted, and furniture updated and organized for efficiency. Every cent must be accounted for. So someone has to go through records with a fine-tooth comb and make sure the budget—past, present, and future—meets military standards. Then every department and every program must give account, answering with results and justifications for why they exist and how they are effective. It's all encompassing, and people's jobs are on the line."

As I type my husband's words, I feel deep conviction. I see the truth of his words in my own lack of accountability. I am three weeks behind in checking my daughter's home school assignments and administering her tests. It's no wonder she's lost motivation. (Not closing the feedback loop has its' negative consequences.)

Not too long ago, I had a conversation with a friend who was the manager in charge of an inspection in the physical therapy department at a nearby hospital. It felt great to finally catch up with him, as he had been working an average of sixty-five hours a week to get ready for the review.

Despite me peppering him with questions about the inspection, he didn't give me many details. I could tell he was tired and just didn't want to think about it at the moment.

Perhaps it would help if I engaged him by explaining *why* I was so interested? "I've always thought it would be so cool if there were some kind of 'family inspection.' You know, a full-on, detailed inspection where every person on the team dedicated themselves to making sure that we had all our t's crossed and i's dotted." I gesticulated wildly with my arms for emphasis, my voice passionate.

He just looked at me and then, after a moment, smiled. You know, the kind of smile that says, *That's nice, but you don't know what you're talking about.*

I pressed on. "What if a third party conducted an investigation in which the physical space had to meet regulation, as well as our budget, our resources, our calendars . . . where we had to give our mission and then answer for results and effectiveness?" I'm sure I exuded intensity. I get a little wild-eyed when I talk about this topic.

"Huh. I hear what you're saying." He paused. "That'd be really hard. Every family has their own way of doing things, their own values and what they deem important."

"Exactly!" I persisted. "But who follows up with them from time to time to see if they're living what they *say* is important to them? Who encourages them to keep up the good work or challenges them to refine their mission and vision? Who coaches them when it's time to check milestones or revise goals?"

In other words: How do you measure success?

Pay Attention to the Milestones

Our family loves a good, old-fashioned road trip. And when I say "old-fashioned," I mean I was *that* mom who decided we wouldn't resort to digital entertainment on road trips. That if looking out the window and watching the world go by was good enough for my grandparents and their children, then it was good enough for us, too.

My aunts and uncles are some of my biggest heroes. Imaginative, funny, witty, resourceful, intuitive, industrious, hard-working, adventurous, playful . . . So part of my strategy in running this corporation (aka: my own family) is to notice the successful qualities in my extended family's cultural heritage and follow suit.

Our children were young when the first portable digital DVD players came out. "Oh well," I'd shrug, when my two oldest pointed out that all their friends watched movies when they went somewhere in the car. "You get to see real life," I countered.

(Actually, I did use technology on our car rides. We listened to cassette tapes and then, later, CDs, including audio books on the topics of leadership, success, a winning attitude, and talks by motivational speakers and leadership gurus.)

For the first fourteen years of our marriage, we lived in Spokane, Washington. Since my family lived in Utah, we made the 692-mile journey about twice a year. We'd stay a week or two and then travel 692 miles back home.

Traveling through the Bitterroot Mountain Range is beautiful. Western Larch, Tamarack, and Cottonwood trees cascade across the mountains. In the autumn, if you squint your eyes while driving past, it looks like the mountain is ablaze. There isn't a time of year in which this part of the country doesn't dazzle the traveler with her scenery. After that, though, the closer you get to Butte, the scenery explains why they call Montana "Big Sky Country." And it's pretty much that way for the remainder of the journey.

And so, we took to watching the mile markers and setting goals to pass the time and "close the feedback loop." If the sign said *13 miles to Pocatello*, we'd take note of the number on the mile marker and then count until we got to the Pocatello Exit sign. Rarely did we take the exit, though. Instead, we'd acknowledge our forward progress, take note of the next milestone, and press on.

When our children were little, we'd start the journey with me holding one hand high in the air and the other down low, like a wide-open crocodile mouth. "This is how far we have to go," I'd tell them. Then, all along the way, every time they asked me how much farther, I'd close the gap accordingly. If they asked me in quick succession so that hardly any distance had passed, I'd demonstrate by keeping my hands the same distance as when they asked only moments ago.

One time, we heard Eli, our oldest, coach his siblings, "Don't ask Mom so soon! Wait for a long time because then when you ask, her hands are a lot closer and that means we've gone a long way!"

As stewards of people development, it's important to cultivate the value of resilience, determination, and resolve in those we lead. To point out the milestones we're moving toward and give feedback along the way.

I realize I run the risk of oversimplifying complex business matters by sharing stories from motherhood. However, I've entertained the (revolutionary?) notion that our work and personal lives might be better served if we blurred the lines between the two. That our legacy is best lived when we're true to our life purpose regardless of our environment.

Whether at work or at home, in our communities or congregations, to be intentional about the story we're telling through our cultures, we need a crystal-clear vision, a roadmap to get there, and milestones to measure progress. Leaders need to ask from time to time, "How does our unique corporate culture follow a plan? Are we committed to the right goals? Do we have a strategy with clear mile markers along the way? How are we closing the feedback loop with efficiency and clarity, providing momentum to our mission?"

When we get out of our own way and take action toward our goals, we build confidence. Success leads to success. And the coolest part? Our success leads others to succeed. Momentum is contagious.

Accountability adds an exponential component of perspective to achieving success in our goals. It's getting someone who's been there, done it, and leads by example, who says, *you've got this. Create your masterpiece. Let's develop your excellence. Here, the expectation is raised. Bring your art. Make an impact. Value your ambition and bring out the ambition in others. Here's how to be contagious and make a difference in the world.* A mentor or coach offers wise feedback, confronts excuses, and asks the right questions to encourage their protégé to dig deep, live from worthiness, and create their most *authentic* legacy.

When our youngest was about seven years old and our oldest was thirteen, my friend Jeri gave me a feedback tip which might bear resemblance to the bonuses given in corporate settings.

"I give my children a quarter for every time they receive a compliment or affirmation on a character quality." She went on to explain how she found this to be a successful way to honor their choices, "to grow in character development, and live out our family's values."

That evening around the dinner table, I told my family we were implementing a new system to honor character development. Since my children were older than her children, I decided on a dollar for every character affirmation. (I humbly acknowledge a dollar is not quite the same as the typical corporate incentives. Adjust as necessary.)

There was only one rule and one caveat. The rule was that it had to be a character affirmation. A compliment on her cute shoes or his nice haircut or a great smile didn't count. Compliments on a firm handshake, looking people in the eyes, asking "investing" questions and listening, those were character affirmations. A dollar for every time someone told me about one of my children doing something that ultimately caused people to feel loved and valued.

The caveat was that we couldn't tell others about this training practice because the knowledge might cause a conflict of interest. We didn't want to inadvertently taint the motives of the person giving the affirmation. The whole point was to enforce our values-driven culture. "And," we told them, "what is done in secret will be rewarded openly." In fact, writing of it in this book is the first time it has been revealed. Although, we stopped practicing this several years ago, since our children got real jobs, earning real paychecks—and the dollar lost its value.

What didn't get lost is the training this provided for our children. Sure, maybe their motives for helping a friend carry her groceries out to the car and wrangle her toddlers into their car seats may have held ulterior motives—at first.

But what we all noticed is that these people, who had no idea that we "paid our children to live out our family's values," were authentically blessed.

The dollar was a tangible way for our children to *see* and *touch* a result even as they *heard* the affirmation. The more of the five senses we engage while learning a habit, the more the habit is reinforced.

It wasn't long before the tangible blessing of the dollar became an inside family something-we-smile-about. But really, it became an *aside*. More and more, we integrated our family values into who we were becoming. Serving others—living beyond ourselves—became the true reward. The highest honor. The legacy we were building.

Over time, I didn't need to have so many one-dollar bills on hand. The habit became their character. They *internalized* the value of living beyond themselves. It became my children's greatest joy to engage in other people's worlds. To give preference. To find a way to give value to every person who crosses their path.

Please don't misunderstand me. Not all the time. I did not invest a wad of one-dollar bills to produce "perfect" children. And they certainly aren't like this all the time when we're at home with only one another. There's been more than a few times that we laughed over something snarky that just came out of a person's mouth after having been complimented thirty minutes before about how they're "always so encouraging." We try to remember not to take ourselves too seriously in the awkward, uncomfortable space of acknowledging the process. Because it *is* a process.

To illustrate a part of this process, let me spare my children for a moment and turn my scrutiny upon myself: I used to be in love with December 31st and January 1st. I suppose I still am, though not as much. I'd invest hours of the last day evaluating the past year and writing down dreams and goals for the year ahead. Then on the first day of the new year, I'd cozy up to the idea of moving forward toward those goals. Heh. "Cozy up." That has never gotten me very far.

One year, I realized I needed checkpoints along the way. So, a few years ago, I fell in love with July 1st. The six-month checkpoint, smack dab in the middle of the year. Last year, I wrote a list of a dozen lofty goals with December 31st as the goal-date for completion. I only succeeded in checking off two. And they were more or less nonnegotiable. As in, they *had* to happen, and we had already found a way to make them work. I didn't have to invest any focused effort or commitment.

Talk about a reality check! I achieved about 16 percent of my goals. Not exactly what I call successful.

Time to reevaluate those checkpoints ... and to establish accountability. Per my success rate, I *desire* to tell one story while the reality is that I'm telling quite a different story.

(Now, I set ninety-day goals, with monthly and weekly checkpoints along the way. And this last year, I invested financially in business coaches. To date, I've tripled and quadrupled my results in several crucial areas of my personal and business life.)

I have an insatiable intrigue with coaching, mentoring, consulting, and other accountability systems designed to bring out the best in people and teams. I gravitate toward reading about them, listening to them, and buying courses from these systems. One of my dreams is to hire a big-name consulting company to come sit around our dining room table in our home and help us develop systems in our "company" to capitalize and leverage our strengths, and strategize for where we need more help. (*It's also my dream to *be* the consulting company who sits around boardroom tables as well as other family's dining room tables developing vision and systems, discovering strengths and creating strategies to achieve goals. Wouldn't that be fun?)

One day, I was on the website of a well-known author, speaker, and owner of such a consulting company. Their company has worked with many big name brands on an international level. On their site, they have a page where companies can apply to have them come to their business for a one- or two-day VIP consultation.

Naturally, I applied.

In the box where it asked the applicant to give a short description of how they might best help, I wrote, "Our family would like to invite your company to sit with us around our dining room table to evaluate our visionary plan. We would like your help to develop systems and strategies and set goals to be more effective in our community and in the world." Then I clicked "submit application."

A couple of months later, I received an email from them stating they would be glad to arrange a meeting with our company. The email included a small handful of packages along with prices. I read through the email, grateful for their response, filed it for posterity's sake, and moved on.

About three months after the email, a representative from their company called me. "We read over your application and would like to pursue this further. Tell me about the service or product your company provides."

Ecstatic to be talking to a real-life business consultant, I gave him our pitch: "Our family strives to love people in such a way as to develop them into their best version of themselves, create community, and deepen relationships so that they live rich, meaningful lives. We're passionate about leadership development and want to learn how to improve in effective business and leadership coaching. I understand your company charges $50,000 for a one-day consulting fee and we believe it's totally worth it—although it's a bit out of our budget at the moment."

Long pause on the other end.

"Hello? Are you still there?" I asked.

"Oh! Yeah, I'm here." Short pause. "Wow, uh, I've never heard of a family wanting to hire a consulting company. I'm not sure how to approach this."

I waited.

"Well," he stammered, "I'll tell you what you can do. Our company sells an online course that sounds like it would be a better fit and more within what you can afford."

I smiled. "Thank you, I appreciate your offer," I said. "I'll make a note of that and perhaps we'll consider it in several months. We're presently working through an online leadership development course so it wouldn't make sense to double up on the same kind of trainings. We're ready to sit down and hash out vision and tactical training with people live and in-person."

"All right, Mrs. Olson. I'll tell you what, we'll call you back in four months, after you're finished with the course you're taking, and we'll talk more then."

I agreed, thanked him for his time, and we hung up.

I sat there mulling over the conversation for a long time. Mulling over the concept of consulting companies who evaluate a business's bottom line and the plan to achieve their goals. Wondering why there aren't companies who consult with *families* on their bottom line and their plan to achieve their goals. How it'd be a tremendous help and gift to have a professional third party sit down with us to brainstorm and construct a framework for success based on our corporate culture and the story we want to tell.

I think they have this in the world already. I think they call it "family counseling." Is the caveat that you must be in a crisis? What if we want to take something good and turn it into excellence?

One such person who sees the value in systems of accountability across industries is Atul Gawande. When I read his book, *Complications*, back in 2002, I immediately found ways to implement concepts from his book into our family structure.

For instance, he wrote about the M&M Conferences that take place in academic hospitals. M&M stands for "Morbidity and Mortality." It's a nonthreatening environment "where doctors can talk candidly about their mistakes." One by one, the past week's cases are reviewed, in detail, and discussed at length as to circumstances, decisions, and consequences.

"The atmosphere at the M&M is meant to discourage both attitudes—self-doubt and denial—for the M&M is a cultural ritual that inculcates in surgeons a 'correct' view of mistakes. 'What would you do differently?' a chairman asks concerning cases of avoidable harm. 'Nothing' is seldom an acceptable answer" (Gawande 2002, 61-62).

"A cultural ritual." Vulnerable, yes. Uncomfortable, definitely. And all at the same time, a culture of embracing our humanness. Our ability to err, and our propensity to learn from mistakes. It's a systematic way to measure success—in a culture that values accountability.

Take Atul Gawande's later book, *The Checklist Manifesto* (2011). Gawande performed an investigation into the effectiveness of checklists to not only avoid catastrophe, but also to improve systems and increase accountability. It's interesting to note that Gawande researched the value of checklists in varying industries such as aviation, surgical medicine, and building construction. What he discovered is that, while checklists are helpful, they have limitations.

At one point, he shadowed construction managers on site. He writes:

> The submittal schedule specified, for instance, that by the end of the month the contractors, installers, and elevator engineers

had to review the condition of the elevator cars traveling up to the tenth floor. The elevator cars were factory constructed and tested. They were installed by experts. But it was not assumed that they would work perfectly. Quite the opposite. The assumption was that anything could go wrong, anything could get missed. What? Who knows? That's the nature of complexity. But it was also assumed that, if you got the right people together and had them take a moment to talk things over as a team rather than as individuals, serious problems could be identified and averted (2011, 66).

Gawande continues:

In the face of the unknown—the always nagging uncertainty about whether, under complex circumstances, things will really be okay—the builders trusted in the power of communication. They didn't believe in the wisdom of the single individual, of even an experienced engineer. They believed in the wisdom of the group, the wisdom of making sure that multiple pairs of eyes were on a problem and then letting the watchers decide what to do.

Man is fallible, but maybe men are less so (2011, 67).

There's something beautiful and strong about cultures that embrace accountability, both within the group as well as from those who offer feedback from the outside.

"They've already been through so much with their first child." The youth director's voice was soft, compassionate. "I'm sorry to see them struggling in their relationships with their younger children, too."

We sat there in the quiet for several long moments. She answered in response to my concerns for a specific family. Discouraged about the fallout in their relationships with their teenagers, they quietly imploded as they tried to keep up appearances while their family spiraled out of control.

We only knew about their circumstances because their children had reached out for help and guidance. The most disconcerting thing was how their relationship with their first child had been rough and the relationships progressively worsened as the family dynamics disintegrated more with each passing year.

We sat there, not saying anything. Because what do you say when you see a family or business which can get support—but steeped in shame and embarrassment, they're afraid to reach out? If we're going to build successful cultures, we must challenge social stigmas. One way to do this is through fostering trust, authenticity, and vulnerability in our personal and business lives. To value transparency and accountability.

We have systems of accountability in surgical theaters, aviation, and building construction. What would it look like to integrate forms of relational accountability in our families, work places, and organizations? How might we implement an M&M Conference *mindset* in *all* the places where we lead? What if our workplaces, schools, communities, and homes thought, *we're building a world class team in this place. By honoring the process and empowering* others with *"a cultural ritual"* which instills a growth mindset, we're developing champions.

One night, our family showed up for a scheduled movie night at our friends', Al and Lisa's, house. Their children answered the door, invited us all in, and ran off to the playroom with our children in tow.

"We're up here," our friends called from the second floor. Curious, we made our way up the narrow staircase to the master suite and bathroom—where they were sitting on opposite sides of their bed, looks of resolve set in their faces. "Well, we're glad you're here. Maybe you can help us work out a solution to this fight we're having."

To this day, I have no idea what their argument was about. What I do remember is thinking, *this is what accountability looks like in a marriage culture. This is what vulnerability and wholeheartedness looks like. This is poetic and messy and beautiful.* I remember we spent the evening sitting on the end of their bed, our conversation ebbing from serious debate to doubled-over laughter.

To this day, they maintain a fun, adventuresome, openhearted—transparent—approach to life. As a result, their marriage and family culture inspires everyone who is fortunate and blessed enough to cross their path.

I heard somewhere that a person's success is determined by how willing he is to engage in hard conversations.

It gets personal at this point. We can't give others what we don't have. This is why I invest time, money, and energy—both emotional and mental—into counselors and mentors. How could I help others live into freedom from shame or fear if I didn't heal in those areas first? How could I help others change their story from defensiveness and people-pleasing unless I learned to face those same issues head on in my own life? Reaching out for help gives me tools and strategies to *practice* a success mindset. Reporting to and receiving feedback from those who are ahead of me and already successful gives me the necessary support to change my perspective. Reaching out makes it possible for me to change my storyboard and live a legacy of freedom instead.

Here's the crux for leaders. Not everyone will seek guidance from a counselor or mentor or coach.

As a result, we leaders need to ask ourselves if we're creating the kind of culture where people feel safe to reach out and be transparent within our organization or family. If, at the end of the day, the people and relationships we invest in are our legacy, then it's worth it to take a careful assessment of our personal and work lives.

By investing in self-development and gaining the skills to connect with others, we can inspire and impact those within our influence. This is how we can revolutionize entire cultures in our personal and professional lives. We can be the Atticus Finch who stands in the gap, gives a voice, and helps others find freedom, too.

It's important to conduct a regular "inspection" in every work place as well as in our personal lives. To have someone from the outside with the competence and passion to follow up on a regular and consistent basis. To check, *How are you doing aligning your actions with your vision?* To give encouragement or help to review the mile markers. To create the narrative that's congruent with the person we dream of becoming.

In his book, *Complications*, Atul Gawande writes about a technique known as "critical incident analysis." It's used in aviation to analyze mishaps. "The technique is built around carefully conducted interviews, designed to capture as much detail as possible about dangerous incidents: how specific accidents evolved and what factors contributed to them. This information is then used to look for patterns among different cases." (2002, 66)

He goes on to say, "Getting open, honest reporting is crucial." (2002, 66)

Feedback is powerful. And to create a safe place where everyone feels secure both giving and receiving feedback, it's important to cultivate a culture that values learning—an environment where everyone knows they're not being judged. Where people embrace the goals of excellence and growth. Accountability.

As a spouse, a parent, friend, how do we measure success in our most important relationships? How do we know we are communicating value and honor and building a foundation of trust in our organizational and family cultures?

Science serves us well when it comes to checklists and "incident analysis" and the plethora of situations from which we can derive hard data. So, when it comes to measuring success in the day-to-day flow of human interactions, how do we stay accountable for growth and meaningful connections?

Value "The Last 10 Percent"

While writing this chapter, I took a break to enjoy Saturday morning brunch with my family. We have a longstanding tradition of Dad-cooks-weekend-brunch around here. This provided the perfect opportunity to get feedback from the team regarding the topic of accountability and feedback.

We've held our own "M&M Conferences" and debriefs in the form of family meetings for years, so I didn't have to elaborate on the concept. Instead, I asked them, "Do you feel safe giving feedback, expressing a concern, or disagreeing in our culture?"

(An aside: I wish you could be part of our family conversations during these moments. It's messy. People talk over one another. They disagree loudly and assertively—sometimes aggressively. They make witty remarks and quote relevant lines from movies. We laugh—a *lot*, as individuals vie for most compelling story or audacious comeback.

Sometimes a line is crossed and someone takes offense and we stop everything to make amends before going on. Truthfully, it's not my style and the chaos can be overstimulating at times. The amazing thing is that I trust these people implicitly. I'd follow them into battle. As messy as it all gets, I know we have each other's backs.)

Effective teams thrive in a culture where honest feedback is rewarded and valued. When I posed the question to my family, they immediately responded with funny movie lines, pithy quotes, and, "Sure, Mom. We know we can be honest."

My husband saved the moment for me, as I'm the introvert who looks for more serious cerebral input. "I think what Mom means, guys, is on a scale of one to ten, with one being 'I don't like receiving negative feedback, I'm really uncomfortable with it,' and ten being 'I enjoy receiving feedback, negative or positive, because I use it to gauge where we're at in a process,' where would you say you're at?"

Then my husband did something brilliant—and rather enlightening. He said, "Wait. Before you answer for yourself, let's give our feedback to one another as to where we think each other is on the scale." Great idea . . . because I would have given myself a ten. However, based on what others perceived of my behavior when receiving negative feedback, my family said I was more of an eight. The same thing occurred as we went around to each person—they rated themselves either a little more open or less receptive in contrast to what others perceived.

And here's what surprised me most: except for me, no one rated anyone else or themselves higher than a five. If you'd asked me if we cultivate a culture of honest and open, grace-based feedback, I would have said an adamant, *yes*. If you had asked me to assess whether we're challenging one another in a way that builds confidence and pushes us out of our comfort zones, I would have said, *absolutely*. Embracing discomfort? Again, *oh, I'm positive we're comfortable with discomfort.* Yet the feedback in real time revealed we have some work to do to build trust. This is the beautiful and uncomfortable mess of reality. It's during these open and honest conversations when we can identify where we're at on the "map" and decide where we'd like to go.

The lesson here: accountability comes in the form of checking in with your people on a regular basis. What are the milestones?

The principle of the last 10 percent is meant to provide space in the relationship where one person can point out another's blind spot. "Hey, that was pretty good work," can be interpreted as, "I'm going to give you 90 percent of the truth, but hold back the last 10 percent of the reality that it was obvious you didn't give it your best."

We've all experienced that moment when someone you care about doesn't play their best game or they sing off-key in a performance or they turn in less than professional work on a project. We have a choice. We can "be nice" and give them a mostly true, "Hey, good game!" or, "I liked the song you chose," or, "Looks good."

It takes a deep level of trust to be in a place where a loved one, friend, or colleague can ask, "Do you want the last 10 percent?" and we're able to listen to what they say. Likewise, we want to know we're relatively safe to step into that vulnerable place of *giving* the last 10 percent.

It's tricky. Apparently, we're a loud bunch. And everyone agreed—amongst the joking and laughing—that we value the last 10 percent. Yet, everyone *also* agreed they don't necessarily feel *safe* hearing and receiving negative feedback.

We say we value taking risks, innovating, and creative problem-solving. Yet, the reality is that 83 percent of the team resorts to behaviors like blame-shifting and defensiveness when confronted.

The stark realization from that meeting was that our foundations of trust are not as sturdy as they need to be to support our family's last 10 percent. I processed this reality and then came back to the family later to propose a plan for getting us back on track with who we want to be as a team. To build an authentic culture of honor, it is crucial to create pathways of communication, free of the debris of shame, fear, and control.

We needed to change the story.

When Accountability Requires Edits to the Script

In the culture of our family, we *acknowledge* the value of the last 10 percent. If someone is lagging or not contributing value or sucking energy from the team, they expect to hear, "Do you want the last ten percent?" or, "Can I point out a blind spot in your life?"

However, as evidenced by the feedback I received at this morning's brunch, we need to craft a different script—one which affirms the courage it takes to feel vulnerable and to step into the messy space where shame tempts us to feel like we're not enough.

It's a process of constantly checking our egos at the door. A process of facing down shame, pushing through fear, and accepting the reality of the way things are. It's exciting and awe-inspiring to rise to the role of screenwriters of our lives.

In the book, *The Complete Book of Scriptwriting*, by J. Michael Straczynski, he writes:

> Nothing is ever obligatory! An attitude of "Well, this scene is expected, and everyone *else* is doing it" can cripple what might otherwise be a fine film. The only thing you as a screenwriter are obliged to do is tell your story. Period. You don't have to follow the standard formula used in *x* number of other films because if you do, then it isn't your script anymore; it's a formula script, and it will never be anything more than that. If you put in one single, solitary, crummy little scene not because you think it belongs there, but because you think it's expected, then forget it. You've just sold out.
>
> There's nothing wrong with a chase scene *if* that scene is an essential part of your story that grows naturally out of the events that precede it. But to do it because it's "obligatory" is just plain dumb. Worse than dumb, in fact, because it's the first step down the road toward losing your integrity as an artist (1996, 143).

That, friends, resonates with every fiber of my being. Whatever our stories are up to this point, if it's not working, then as artists, we mustn't sell out. It's our responsibility to stay true to the vision. The experiments and risks that don't quite work for the story we're telling? We'll muster the courage to accept they're not working, allow ourselves to feel the disappointment, and then relegate them to the "outtakes."

This one life here on earth is too precious to look around, see how everybody else's "films" play out, only to shrug apathetically and settle for status quo.

The liberating reality is that we can live a life worthy of a blockbuster. That all these moments are opportunities to exceed current limits.

Honestly? As jarring as it is to hear someone point out our blind spots—to receive the last 10 percent—it might be just the *oomph* we need to get us out of the proverbial rut.

The Power of "And, Also . . ."

After serious introspection, I can see where my leadership falls short when it comes to encouraging experimentation. Far too often, I hear an idea and react with, "Yes, but . . ." I stop a possibility short by giving feedback that throws water, instead of fuel, on the fire. It grieves me to know that I've gotten in the way instead of empowering those around me.

Right now, I'm recommitting to cultivating an "And, also . . ." culture. Taking that knee-jerk response of self-preservation, that

"Yes, but . . ." and changing it to an invitation for development, for dreaming. An "And, also . . ." is such a small change—just two words! But the change it invites—*implementation*—is profound indeed.

Wise leaders work to create cultures where people feel safe giving and receiving feedback. They reach out, ask questions, and invite those around them to hold them accountable.

If the idea of inviting accountability—or a deeper level of accountability—into your personal and work life sounds intimidating or threatening, let me ask you a hard question: What is your end goal?

Allow me to be rhetorical . . . Is your goal to feel good, get kudos and strokes? Or do you want to grow, and in the process, help people, and commit to a legacy that outlives your life? The fact that you're reading this book leads me to believe it's the latter. Your commitment to the latter means you can get excited about receiving the gift of accountability as you dream audacious dreams and set outrageous goals.

Cultures where people embrace accountability and feedback are spaces that nurture and fuel innovation, growth, and learning. Which is where we're headed in the next chapter.

6. A Culture of Exploration

Go on failing. Go on. Only next time, try to fail better.
—Samuel Beckett, Irish writer

"Failure is not fatal."

This coming from a mentor who lives bold and daring. His audacious love and authentic care for people combined with professionalism and work ethic have made him a trusted leader in his community.

Community sounds a bit small in his case. His influence stretches throughout the region. Larry Templeton invests the moments of his days into making this side of eternity sweeter for those in his sphere of influence. Not just sweeter, also more meaningful. He does this practically as well as through his interactions.

By trade, Larry is an investment and insurance agent. In the more than thirty years that he's run his company, he has traveled tens of thousands of miles to help people make wise financial decisions. But Larry's true success comes by way of the passion and wisdom he brings to every conversation.

He asks great questions and he listens intently. He takes notes. Then he asks more penetrating questions. He's interested, not just because he's trying to discern how to best help—though that's certainly a part of it—but because he's truly invested in the person in front of him.

One time, my husband and I called him when our marriage hit a rough patch and we needed a "tune-up." That evening around the dining table, he asked questions, listened, and shared insights from his experiences. I don't know how he does it. There, in the middle of a not-so-fun season, he had us laughing as he shared stories from his own marriage. His keen sense of humor and transparency communicated *this is an opportunity to learn and grow.*

Another time, he showed up at my front door, randomly, without calling ahead—not his normal practice. That particular day was weighing heavy on me as I battled depression and discouragement.

"I just had a feeling that I needed to stop by and ask if everything is okay. Is there something you need to talk about?"

I stood there, quiet. Tears spilled onto my cheeks as I confessed a sense of hopelessness and defeat. I caught him up on the last few months, as we hadn't spoken in a while. He listened compassionately before reassuring me there was healing and restoration for a soul battered and overwhelmed. He shared a couple of resources with me that had helped him in the past when he went through similar experiences.

And then, still standing there on the porch (I think I forgot to invite him in, since he was only "stopping by"), he prayed hope and confidence and restoration over me.

Dozens of instances and conversations with Larry, such as this one, cause me to believe that he's one of the most fearless—and creative—people I know.

Larry and his wife, Sherri, are one of those dynamic couples who demonstrate a marriage culture full of learning, exploration, and fun. Together, they're going through life not so focused on what they're going to achieve as they are focused on asking, "What will we learn?"

Have you ever spent time in the presence of someone who so thoroughly, so passionately lives in the moment that you found yourself lost in the moment with them? Those people whose love is so genuine, so pure, that places opened in your soul that you didn't even know existed? Somehow, they create space for others to think creatively. To be bolder. More courageous. It's beautiful. Larry Templeton is like that.

In our family, we call these people Energy Givers. "Be an Energy Giver!" is the exhortation.

Liz Wiseman of the Wiseman Group calls them "Multipliers." Erwin Raphael McManus reminds us we're "Artisan Souls." In fact, in his book, *The Artisan Soul*, he writes, "Creativity should be an everyday experience. Creativity should be as common as breathing. We breathe, therefore we create" (2014, 5). To some, that might sound idealistic. However, I'm on a mission to help people stop settling for broken systems and instead live a story—a *legacy*—ignited with passion, creation, hope, joy, empathy, adventure, growth, meaning, grit, impact, connection, (our vocabulary for *ambition*).

Wired for Exploration

Families and companies which tell a story of creativity and innovation value curiosity and nurture wonder. They foster cultures that develop leading learners.

I heard a story once about a mom and her precocious son. When he was three years old, he declared that he was done with his crib and ready for a "big boy bed." His mother told him something to the effect of "Soon enough."

The next day she found him with a screwdriver, busy dismantling his crib. Joining him on the floor, she helped him take apart the crib. That night he slept in a "big boy bed." Apparently, there were many stories like this throughout the boy's childhood. And each time, his mother did her best to support his ideas. Eventually, that boy, Jeff Bezos, grew up and started Amazon.com out of his garage.

Each of us is equipped to bring solutions to the challenges in the world. But to do so, we need to be courageous enough to dismantle old paradigms, break traditions, and embrace the learning curve innate with every creative venture.

Recently, our family had a brainstorming session. These conversations are always a perfect mixture of intensity and fun. *Intense* because the dreams are way beyond us and *fun* because it stimulates our imaginations and gets us thinking about the possibilities. We believe that if our dreams don't scare us, they're probably too small and too safe. Sometimes our brainstorming sessions are focused on one topic. Other times, we're all over the place, conceptualizing ideas that lead to ideas that *might* lead to a breakthrough idea. What's important is that we drive these sessions with a vision for possibilities in the future.

These times infuse our family with renewed anticipation and energy. They take the "best that we can hope for" and help us visualize how we might transform hopes into realities that make a meaningful, lasting impact.

The world needs more Energy Givers who help those around them envision possibilities and take risks. Energy Givers are contributors. They create. We're forever telling our people they have possibility inside them that has the potential to make a difference in someone else's life. And while I don't believe this life is a dress rehearsal—it's the real deal—I do believe in the value of practice. As in, practice doing the next thing. In fact, as I got a few chapters into this book, I started to experience self-doubt. Lots. So much in fact that, terrified, I entertained the thought of giving up the idea of writing a book altogether. Then the words I've preached, whispered back to me.

Practice. Not perfection. Practice.

Embrace Improvisation

In his book, *Blink*, Malcolm Gladwell describes the science of improvisation. "It involves people making very sophisticated decisions on the spur of the moment, without the benefit of any kind of script or plot. That's what makes it so compelling and—to be frank—terrifying" (2007, 113). He continues, "What is terrifying about improv is the fact that it appears utterly random and chaotic.

It seems as though you have to get up onstage and make everything up, right there on the spot. But the truth is that improv isn't random and chaotic at all" (2007, 113).

Larry Templeton gave me the best business advice I've ever received, "Sharon, take action." He reassured me in his forthright way, "You'll learn from your failures and mistakes. If you don't take action, you won't fail. But you won't learn, and you won't make progress on your goals either."

This is where I remind myself to breathe. To remember I don't have to stand on life's proverbial stage and "make everything up, right there on the spot." When we show up for our lives, take risks, and embrace the process, we get to learn what Gladwell refers to as "a series of rules."

Gladwell writes, "Improv is an art form governed by a series of rules, and they want to make sure that when they're up onstage, everyone abides by those rules . . . How good people's decisions are under the fast-moving, high-stress conditions of rapid cognition is a function of training and rules and rehearsal" (2007, 113-114).

I've been to improv shows and witnessed the uncomfortable awkwardness when someone's line fell flat or an action didn't work within the context of the scene. And this is what makes me love improv: there's a moment of self-effacing laughter, lighthearted banter, and then the show goes on. Sometimes they back up a few lines. Usually, they pick up where they left off.

"One of the most important of the rules that make improv possible, for example, is the idea of agreement, the notion that a very simple way to create a story—or humor—is to have characters accept everything that happens to them . . . [improvisers create] the conditions for successful spontaneity." (2007, 114). I love that.

What if our lives more closely resembled the rules in improv?

Show up. Accept everything that happens. (Remember, the definition of integrity is "having the courage to meet the demands of reality.") How might we change our stories if we reframed the scenes of our lives with grace and humor?

In thinking about why improv works, I realized one of the criteria for success is emotional integrity. The scenes take unexpected turns, but the best improvisors master the art of navigating with humility, flexibility, and transparency. They step into the scene, fully present, leading with confidence and authenticity.

While sitting in the audience of an improv show, I noticed no one stresses when the lines or actions don't work. No one gets frustrated or frazzled. In fact, there were times when the scene got so ridiculous that the improvisors on stage lost their composure. In giving themselves permission to embrace the messiness of the moment, they doubled over in laughter, which rippled out over the audience.

These are the scenes we attach at the end of a movie and label them outtakes. What if we came at life as Improvisors and allowed more outtakes? More scenes filled with hilarity? What if we didn't expect ourselves and those around us to show up polished and rehearsed? What if we embraced the process of mastery and practiced setting the scene for "successful spontaneity"? How might this create a culture of Energy Givers where the expectation is that we're creating a story together?

Energy Givers don't try to change people or circumstances. They change the story by working on themselves. They invest in self-development so they can contribute more value to others. Energy Givers adapt, bringing the best of who they are to the moment, confident as leading learners. As a result, they energize others and bring out the best in those around them.

Exploring this concept of improv theater challenged me to think about my own propensity to control—read, *change*—the scenes in my life. Growing in maturity has meant more than learning to *roll with it, pull myself up by my bootstraps, let go*, or any of the other trite phrases we use to console ourselves when life is hard.

It means learning to *embrace the suck*, as my two oldest sons, Eli and Isaiah, put it. It means *accepting* everything that happens to me.

It means practicing responses that align with my principles, values, and vision. The more I show up for life's "rehearsals," the more adept I become at creative problem solving and innovating. I'm learning to be brave. Not just brave, but I'm learning to lean into the unexpected with grace and humor, courage and conviction, purpose and authenticity.

Hal Elrod, international speaker, author of the bestselling *Miracle Morning* series, and creator of the Miracle Morning revolution, states the idea of "accepting everything that happens to me" as "The Five-Minute Rule." He gives himself five minutes to process negative emotions when things take an unexpected turn. But after five minutes, he accepts reality for what it is, and figures out the best way to move forward.

The idea that "... decisions are made under the fast-moving, high-stress conditions of rapid cognition is a function of training and rules and rehearsal," was evidenced in the way Hal faced one of the most difficult circumstances in his life. Driving home from a company event where he had just received an award for being their top salesman, he was hit by a drunk driver head-on at seventy miles per hour, then immediately hit on the driver's side door by another car that didn't have time to swerve. Dead for six minutes at the scene and then in a coma for six days, when he awoke the doctors told him he had permanent brain damage and he might never walk again. Faced with an unfathomable reality, Hal drew from his "training and rehearsal" of the Five-Minute Rule. After thinking it through, he decided he'd either learn to walk again or he'd be the happiest person in a wheelchair.

Improvisors tend to be happy people. They acknowledge there's no value in dwelling on something that's already happened. They're able to bring their energy and creativity to the moment, *well, that just happened. Okay, let's figure this out.* This doesn't minimize the pain or stress of life's hard scenarios. It enables and empowers us to not get stuck, ultimately giving us the gift of emotional freedom.

Hal did learn to walk again. In fact, he went on to run a fifty-two-mile ultra marathon. He now travels internationally as a life coach and speaker for schools and corporate events.

Marie Forleo, entrepreneur and founder of B-School, says everything is figureoutable. I agree.

Life is full of unexpected moments. Problems arise. Things don't always turn out like we envisioned. Being uncomfortable is . . . well, *uncomfortable*. The only way to change the trajectory of the story is to walk through the discomfort. And to keep walking until you get to the other side.

Remember, failure isn't fatal. Improvise. Be an Energy Giver by accepting what is and contributing your ideas for turning the storyline. Don't give in to blame shifting or replaying the scene over and over, wishing it were different (a temptation I battle all too frequently). Instead, separate yourself from the adversity and try something different. Maybe it'll work. Maybe it won't. Keep moving.

You must be relentless about "doing stuff." That's what Isaiah, our nineteen-year-old, declares constantly. New York Times Bestselling Author and Lead Pastor of National Community Church, Mark Batterson says, "The antidote for the fear of failure is not success but small doses of failure."

Go. Do. Stuff.

It's in the creative expressions when we show up for life and when we're interacting with others that we find our unique, brave contribution.

Our deepest fear is not that we are inadequate. Our deepest fear is that we are powerful beyond measure. It is our light, not our darkness, that most frightens us. We ask ourselves, "Who am I to be brilliant, gorgeous, talented, fabulous?" Actually, who are you not to be? You are a child of God. Your playing small doesn't serve the world. There is nothing enlightened about shrinking so that other people won't feel insecure around you. We are all meant to shine, as children do. We were born to make manifest the glory of God that is within us. It's not just in some of us; it's in everyone. And as we let our own light shine, we unconsciously give other people permission to do the same. As we're liberated from our own fear, our presence automatically liberates others.

—Marianne Williamson

Watch One. Do One. Teach One.

There's a mantra used by students going through residency in teaching hospitals: *Watch one. Do one. Teach one.*

That's a brilliant philosophy if you're trying to build a culture where everyone feels empowered to explore, problem solve and come up with creative solutions.

Nurture a culture that says, "Watch. Like this."

And then, "Now you do it."

Celebrate progress. Celebrate steps. Cheer for each other. Not because it's done perfect. Or because they replicated exactly what was taught. But because it fosters creativity.

And then: "Now go teach someone else."

The Value of Rehearsals

When our children were little, we practiced everything. Bedtime, leaving (the house as well as other places), delayed gratification, using a soft tone of voice, character qualities, going to the grocery store. Nothing was out of bounds for rehearsal. Our own little fire drills.

For instance, greeting people and dignifying their personhood was nonnegotiable. We didn't use the labels *shy* or *bashful* in our home. Did our children still duck their heads, avert their eyes, or hide behind us when an adult friend engaged with them? Yes, it happened. But we didn't tolerate it and we didn't justify it as a personality or temperament trait. We taught them the importance of *seeing* people. Really seeing them.

"Look people in the eyes," we'd tell them. Then we'd model the behavior we wanted. We looked intently into our children's eyes and said, "I see you. And I love you."

Too many workplaces function with supervisors and employees who lack confidence and customer service skills. Besides an inability to bring the best of who they are to the customers, they leave relational carnage within the workspace. They're energy *takers*. Micromanagement, distrust, power plays, and territorialism stifle creativity, learning, and growth. Beyond the emotionally volatile environment, it affects the bottom line.

One of my core convictions is that people can *learn* to interact another way. Remember, a culture will follow the storyline being told unless someone speaks up and interjects, "Wait. We don't have to keep this plotline. We can edit and revise."

It may be someone within the company or it may be a coach or consultant hired to come in and oversee the storyboard rewrite: What is the story this company wants to create? Who are we? What is this for?

What is our vision and how can we align our values to get us there?

It takes courage and conviction to be the only one in the 'classroom' who sees an injustice and has the audacity to go against the status quo to make something right. Or to lead the culture from surviving to thriving.

Yes, we taught our children to give people a firm handshake, look them in the eye, acknowledge them by learning their name... We also taught them to be dangerous. In the culture of our family this meant not being nice in the traditional sense of pleasantries for the sake of looking good. We taught them life is too short to be self-serving. That it's far better to love big and bold and risk getting your heart broken than to hold back, "be nice," and play small.

Nothing is more important on the face of this Earth than people. We emphasized it over and over. Then, when the "improv" moment presented itself, we'd encourage our children to practice seeing people, acknowledging them, listening, and therefore, showing value.

Of course, we couldn't script every scenario they might possibly encounter, and we're far from having it perfect, but they know the principles. They can draw from the training, rules, and rehearsals.

How might our workspaces, communities, and schools be better if we all practiced more vulnerability, more authenticity, more empathy? If we lived more openhearted?

People don't take me seriously when I tell them I'm a natural introvert because I behave like an extrovert. Integrity and growth dictated that I come to terms with the question, *Am I introverted, or am I being rude? Am I using my preference for quiet, reflective spaces as an excuse to be self-absorbed?* I practiced striking up conversations with strangers, asking meaningful questions, listening. I'm *still* practicing. Rehearsing. In my goal to become a better conversationalist (and to conquer my fear of public speaking), I joined Toastmasters International.

I also invested in a Mastermind group for entrepreneurs—one of the best investments I've made to date. The facilitator, Austin Netzley, author of *Make Money, Live Wealthy*, and creator of *Six-Figure Author* is a brilliant example of what it looks like to be an expert listener as well as a connector. He's mastered the art and skill of *seeing* people, drawing out potential, and getting everyone in the group to collaborate and contribute to one another's success. It's an invaluable and incredible experience to interact with those who are playing at a higher level. I'm being stretched far out of my comfort zone as I'm called on to speak up and contribute my ideas to other's success.

What will we solve? What will we create? What will we learn?

In doing work that matters, we must think into what could be. In *Artisan Soul*, Erwin McManus writes, "We are most human when love is our motive. It is the same with creativity. God . . . designed us to dream, to risk, and to create" (2014, 11-12).

This is an area of our family's culture where we've struggled. Eli, our oldest, told me recently that to be creative, there needs to be a sense of empowerment.

Too often, my husband and I have found ourselves bound by the desire for control. In our earnest desire to keep things neat and tidy (read "perfect"), we squelched creativity.

My friend, Alice, is teaching her two-year old daughter to think critically—to think creatively by considering options. She or her daughter will strike up a conversation with a suggestion for something they could do . . . "Let's go on a walk." And Alice will respond with, "Or . . ." To which her daughter will suggest going in the backyard. And Alice will say, "Or . . ." And Brooklyn will say, "We can read."

Alice might say, "Or . . ." three or four times before asking which one her daughter chooses. What if we all practiced this a little more? When presented with a scenario that has us feeling stuck, out of options, and up against the wall, we might ask ourselves, "Or . . ." We can experiment, improvise, be spontaneous.

Seth Godin, bestselling author and entrepreneur, teaches the importance of being able to accept, "This might not work."

In *Artisan Soul*, McManus presents the case for creating into the future with eloquence: "The past will be our future until we have the courage to create a new one. To make our lives a creative act is to marry ourselves to risk and failure" (2014, 7).

Oh, how I desire to build a risk-taking culture where the people within our influence are empowered to create solutions to the world's problems!

> *Fail! If you're not failing, you've stopped dreaming.*
> *You'll eventually stop learning. And you will stop growing.*
> —Craig Groeschel

Our four children would return from long afternoons of building their fort in the forest, eyes gleaming, stomachs hungry, and imaginations brimming with stories. One day, there was all the usual tumbling in and talking over one another to tell the stories of their adventures, except there was that edge of it-was-dangerous-but-we-survived.

The older two spoke in animated voices: "Mom! It was so much fun! And a little scary. But mostly awesome. Look at the scrapes on Zeke's stomach and chest!"

Zeke pulled up his shirt to reveal what looked like three bear claw scratches, only not as deep. They ran the length of his torso from his upper chest down to a couple of inches below his ribs.

Given that he wasn't bleeding profusely and he wasn't in distress, I breathed relief and settled in to hear the story.

"Zae and Zeke were working on the high platform, about twelve feet up, when I heard a lot of cracking sounds." Eli took a couple of apple slices from the plate in front of him, holding them while he told the story. His whole face was wild with excitement. "Then I looked over and saw them both in a big pile on the ground."

Zae chimed in, "We were just sitting up there, hammering wood pieces, when the whole thing crashed below us."

"And then I got these." Zeke studied the scratches with fascination.

"What an adventure!" This is my standard go-to statement for when I am genuinely excited to hear about their amazing adventure . . . *and* for when my Mama instincts kick in and I'm a little freaked out by their story but don't want them to know.

"We need to go back and rebuild that platform," Zae said, his demeanor fervent.

I held a straight face. "Huh. What do you have in mind?"

"Mom! You don't have to worry." Eli put his hand up as if to stop my worry midstream—apparently, my face wasn't straight enough. "We figured out a different way to make sure it will hold next time!"

If we're intent on creating a culture of doing work that matters, we need to relentlessly sustain attitudes of perpetual optimism. Yes, failures along the way are inevitable. And, failure isn't fatal.

Of course, I'm speaking in generalities, but children seem to be naturals at creating, aren't they? They show up for life exuberant, faith-filled and ready to improvise.

Whoa. Hold on. Maybe not the improvise part. At least, *I* didn't have any toddlers willing to improvise when things didn't go their way. Turns out, we *learn* an Improvisation mindset. So be it. Let's learn by watching those who are masters. Let's rehearse successful spontaneity. Then, let's teach others. Watch one. Do one. Teach one.

7. The Legacy of a Community

Call it a clan, call it a network, call it a tribe, call it a family:
Whatever you call it, whoever you are, you need one.
—Jane Howard

"What is life like for you?"

"Where are you at?"

Sometimes, where we're at, is living a legacy that doesn't look at all like the one we'd prefer to live. It's lonely and sometimes even a little embarrassing. Or the pain is deep. And we don't want to burden anyone so we're careful about how much of ourselves we share. Besides, transparency looks too risky. Too vulnerable. So we self-soothe, determined to figure it out, and over time we find ourselves looking for the page where we can choose another adventure, but we feel stuck in the one we're in. Ever been there?

If you're like me, you've experienced both the surrealism of standing in the middle of an impossible dream-come-true as well as the moment of disillusionment when it feels as though the breakthrough will never come. When those moments turn into seasons, they can be both dream-killers and passion-thieves. I've asked people, "What are you passionate about?" and received a glazed-over expression, their voice monotone, as they told me they had zero passion, that they couldn't even define passion. I get it. I've been there—more than once.

Before we can have the determination, conviction, courage, and sheer grit it takes to pursue dreams, impact our world, and lead with both vision and passion, we need to be honest about where we are . . .

When Hope is Deferred

One of the darkest seasons of my life was a three-year period of stagnancy. Paralyzed by past failures and unforgiveness, I spiraled into a self-deprecating depression where survival became the order of the day. My soul dwindled as I settled into a place of complacency. A place void of passion.

Our souls crave congruence. And when our heart and our brain aren't aligned, it's easy to seek solace in self-preserving behaviors. In other words, we often tell ourselves, *I know I need to take better care of myself. I need to eat healthier and exercise.* Or, *I know I ought to take time for introspection. I know I need to nurture my dreams and make an action plan to achieve my goals. I know I need to pay better attention to my finances—to be more intentional.* We *know* a lot in our minds.

However, we *live* from our hearts.

Therefore, all the knowing in the world won't give us the freedom and fulfillment that comes from living out of wholeheartedness. Neuroscientists call it our subconscious. I particularly like what author and cognitive neuroscientist, Dr.

Caroline Leaf, calls it: the heart-brain. It's in the "heart-brain" where we store all our memories and our perceptions of those memories.

I had always focused on the parts of my growing up years that were dreamy and idyllic, believing I had relinquished the not-so-amazing parts to some out-of-the-way corner of my life, more of an annoyance than anything.

Then, right around my thirtieth birthday, a series of events occurred which revealed some ugly, jagged pieces of my heart. Sure, we can leverage circumstances to build our character, but they also *reveal* areas in our heart-brains—our subconscious—where there might be unresolved matters. The latter was the case in this instance. Where time and proximity had provided a buffer between me and some toxic relationships, I unwittingly invited these people into our home. The foundation of these relationships was a profound sense of fear and shame.

Suddenly, no one met my expectations. Least of all, myself. And since I was so deeply disappointed in myself for not meeting my own expectations, I figured everyone else must be disappointed in me, too.

Rage welled up in me and I'd explode over trivial matters. The budget didn't balance to the penny and in a tirade, I'd yell. Important papers would get moved or misplaced and I'd clench my fists and lecture loudly on the importance of respect. (Yes, I know. The irony and hypocrisy.) The smallest things sent me reeling.

My grown children remember the time I grabbed our "Family Mission Statement" from off the mantel and threw it on the ground, the mangled frame and broken shards of glass a symbol of what my unhealed heart and rage were doing to my family.

Frustrated with myself and determined to gain control of my emotions, I told my closest friends that I was falling apart. That I couldn't "keep it together."

The rage masked deeper underlying matters of the heart. Inner vows made long before—*I will never be like so-and-so, I will never be sick or play into the scarcity mindset, I will never be a victim*—played on a continuous loop in my mind. Yet, no matter how desperately I tried to control the details of my life, I consistently behaved like the people I said I'd never be like. I felt as though I lived in a dark pit, the sides covered in oily residue so that no amount of trying to get a grip to climb out did any good. Although LeRoy made more than a sufficient income and all our needs were met, I worried all the time, obsessing over the budget. Overcome with negative emotions and wallowing in despair, I existed in a pit I couldn't climb out of myself.

One day, a friend and mentor told me that depression is anger turned inward. Although insights like this were a far cry from a cure-all, they acted as a trail of divine breadcrumbs leading me home. Small aha! moments from mentors, counselors, and friends gave me what I needed to ponder on the road to emotional freedom.

What I didn't know then, but now understand, is that those inner vows we make . . . become our reality.

Caught in a vicious cycle of fear, shame, and control, LeRoy and I defaulted to patterns of codependency. Rather than take responsibility for our own lives, we violated one another's boundaries in an effort to "fix" the deficiencies we perceived in the other. My friend, Heather, told me one day that she got a picture of "tending to one another's garden, instead of taking care of the weeds in our own garden."

Toxic beliefs filled the voids as I slipped into an obsession with my appearance and performance. I alternated between fad diets and binge eating, using food (or the self-deprivation thereof), to try to gain some sense of control. I took on more responsibilities, saying yes to every "opportunity" until I had zero margin in my life for quiet and reflection. And for a long season, we lost our way.

The classic analogy of crabs in a bucket described our marriage. When crabbing, a lid isn't necessary over the bucket of crabs. For, when a crab happens to grab the top of the bucket to climb out, the crabs below him will pull him down, back into the bucket. Fraught with fear and shame, anytime one of us turned in the pursuit of freedom, the other was there to pull down, making sure we stayed in the bucket of mediocrity and complacency together.

This is the murky path I walked. Dr. Henry Cloud describes it as the "Three-Corner Roundabout" in his book, *The Power of the Other* (2016, 50). There's the first corner in which we hold back, resist reaching out, remaining disconnected from any form of intimacy or transparency.

In this corner, I determined, I can fix this on my own. I can get a handle on this. I dug deep and strengthened my resolve, albeit, solitary resolve.

But that corner gets lonely after a while, so we move to Corner Two where, somehow, we find ourselves unwittingly in unsafe relationships in which we're never good enough. It's not (usually) intentional, but these relationships "have the power to make you feel bad" (2016, 40).

And this second corner? Well, the human spirit can only handle feeling inferior for so long.

Eventually, we move into Corner Three, and in search of something to make us feel better after feeling bad for so long, we imbibe in dopamine-releasing gratifications, albeit temporary, "fixes." Food, performance, control . . .

In hindsight, I see how I circled this roundabout—first, isolating myself, then gravitating toward unhealthy relationships. Finally, in an attempt to numb the shame and feelings of not being enough, I'd devour a piece of triple-layer chocolate cake and think, *This is my legacy? Sheesh, this script feels hopeless. I was sure there was more to this story. I've always known there's more. I'll try harder. I can figure out a way to prove to myself and others that I'm enough.* At last, ashamed, and self-berating over my *lack* of everything I perceived as necessary to succeed, I'd return to Corner One, isolating myself once again.

I was miserable.

And yet, those divine breadcrumbs were saving graces.

In the midst of the journey, I picked up Stephen R. Covey's audio book, *The 7 Habits of Highly Effective People*, and listened to it on an eleven-hour road trip. This is what began my quest for building a culture of honor in our home. A quest that would become the driving force behind defining our mission and would eventually evolve into aligning our story with our core values. I didn't realize it at the time, but as I set out to heal our home, I also set in motion the healing of my heart.

Second, LeRoy and I were given the gift of an eighteen-week parenting class. At the time, we thought it was to train us to be better parents. And it did. But now I see that, sometimes, we need to be re-parented ourselves.

During those eighteen weeks, we engaged with ten other people—a single grandmother raising her three grandchildren, a single mom trying to maintain her sobriety from a drug addiction, a sweet young couple in which the dad obtained a pass to leave jail temporarily to attend class, along with others. Over the weeks, our ragamuffin group listened to each other's narratives.

We formed a community around the shared goal of living a purposeful legacy instead of a reactive legacy. A shared goal of changing our stories to living from a place of nurture and kindness—first to ourselves, knowing the overflow would splash onto our spouses, our children, and others.

Honestly? At times, it did feel a little kumbaya-ish. After all, on various levels, every person in our group needed to recover from the addiction of the three-corner roundabout. But slowly, over the weeks, our heart-brain circuitries were being rewired. We set goals and celebrated each other's successes the following week. (Yep, just like in a sobriety meeting.) We were given tools to help us communicate better with our spouse as well as with our children. We learned to reframe hard moments as challenges instead of as a threat. We became more generous as we gave ourselves grace when we didn't quite live up to our own expectations . . . And, as our hearts healed, the affects rippled into the lives of our children.

Grace upon grace, slowly over time, we were given the building blocks to stop leaving emotional shrapnel as our legacy and instead become the visionary leaders our children needed us to be. We forgave ourselves, let go of the past, and looked forward, aligning our beliefs with our vision of what was yet to be.

And finally, (a grace which remained solid throughout the struggle), we were intimately connected with a community of people who continued to challenge us. We reached out and asked a couple whose marriage was about ten years ahead of us, to mentor us. I continued to ask women further ahead in their journey, for counsel. And we had one key mentor who continued to pull out the best in us—really, to plug us into leadership roles where serving and loving people transcended our difficult circumstances.

Michael Hockett was one of the administrative pastors in our faith community at the time. Under his leadership, we facilitated workshops on parenting and—yes, marriage. We continued to mentor engaged couples (which always provided some intense self-analysis . . . maybe that was the point?). We also led the Married Couples Night Out group—a twice-a-month date night for parents with young children. (And those "mandatory" date nights—because the leaders had to set the example, right?—acted as a saving grace.)

All the while, we were honest and transparent with our mentors and those closest to us about our struggles. We kept reaching out and they, in turn, refused to give up on us. Michael relentlessly saw more in us than we saw in ourselves. While connecting us with mentors to guide us, he saw areas in our lives where we were already successful and continued to put us in places where we were called on to mentor others in their journey.

Energy Givers like Michael Hockett are leaders who don't accept excuses, looking instead for tangible ways to empower and develop the potential in those they lead. They acknowledge the reality of a "terrible-two tantrum" while standing back, separate, from the situation in front of them. They hold their emotions in check so they can speak life and dignity and possibility into the moment. They know people can change, so they raise the standards and give encouragement to help people acknowledge false, limiting beliefs and change their mindsets.

I remember a disheartening conversation with a friend in which she shared something she heard at a conference about the human *in*ability to change. Bursting with enthusiasm and conviction, she told me the speaker's credentials and then related to me the stories she heard that reiterated her belief. At the end of her story she looked at me and sighed with relief. She said this explained why no matter how much she tried, change was impossible.

Change is hard. Anyone? And while we acknowledge the *discomfort* of change, the idea that we can't change couldn't be further from the truth. Our mindsets can change. Our brains can improve and get healthier.

How many people are going about in a zombie-like state, stuck in limiting beliefs because they don't think change is possible? Entire branches of science and research are devoted to the discovery of *how* we implement change. Psychologist, Carol Dweck, wrote a masterpiece on this topic. Her book, *Mindset,* delves deep into the science of people who have what she calls a "fixed mindset" and those with a "growth mindset."

People with a fixed mindset are those who believe people don't, or can't, change. This is common in families or within friendships in which people have known each other for a long time. *You're taking up cooking? We all know you can barely boil a pot of water.* Or, *you're suddenly into travel? I thought you didn't like traveling.* Please hear me when I say, people can and do change.

Those with a growth mindset get excited when they see people around them stretch out of their comfort zone and expand their horizons. They understand the challenges of learning and mastering a new skill set and they dig deep, embrace reality, and implement an attitude of fortitude. They don't allow themselves to be victims to the tyranny of fear and doubt. Instead, they stay the course, trusting the process.

One of my missions during my stint on this ball of dirt, is to help people break free from false beliefs that hold them in bondage from emotional, spiritual, mental, physical, and financial freedom. It is one of my core convictions that people can change. We can write a different story with more meaningful, vision-oriented impact.

I know what it's like to endure difficult seasons and find freedom. I witnessed the incredible breakthrough of overcoming obstacles and experiencing real change. I get what it's like to emerge from the valley with passion renewed—especially after working so hard for something I believed in. And our community confirmed that it's absolutely crucial to be surrounded by those with a growth mindset, who fuel energy and passion on the road to *becoming* people who live a legacy of authenticity, confidence, courage, and conviction. But I'm getting ahead of myself . . .

Our breakthrough came when Michael asked us to teach a session at an upcoming marriage retreat. Fueled by our passion to see marriages live out their full potential (and believing it was entirely possible for us, too), we said yes. For the next four months, LeRoy and I faced the reality of our own messy story even as we prepared to encourage approximately sixty other couples.

For four painful months, we fought and cried and got more honest and vulnerable with each other than in a long, long time. But we laughed, too. As we came up with the points we felt were important, and the stories to illustrate, we were reminded of what's truly important. Egos began softening as a genuine desire for emotional authenticity and transparency filled the space between us.

Getting beyond oneself to engage in serving others, especially when pursued alongside others, can act as a catalyst for healing. In the transcendent experience of getting out of our comfort zone together, we were forced to examine the current narrative we were telling and reshape the culture of our marriage to align with our mission.

And our speaking engagement? I recall looking over at LeRoy during our seventy-five-minute session and feeling love, respect, and admiration for him on a level I'd never experienced. We had fought hard to get through this valley. I remember thinking, *This. This is what we're made for . . . people investors.*

Isn't this the way of it? Stuck in the mire of shame or fear or control (or a combination of those), we can either choose to keep circling the roundabout, or we can decide to move to a healthier, more wholehearted place. A place where passion is alive and well. However, to go there, we need to get honest about our emotions, take ownership, and recognize the stories we're telling about them.

Sometimes our stories demand relentless editing.

Ours did.

Through the experience of scripting encouragement for other couples, we stopped pulling each other down and started emotionally hoisting and supporting one another in our separate journeys out of complacency—essentially writing encouragement into our own script. By joining forces in a quest bigger than us, we reconnected with our mission to invest in people—igniting a cultural shift in our marriage and renewing our vision.

It wasn't that everything was suddenly fixed. But it's the epic tale of the protagonists who go up against a formidable challenge. They accept, they struggle together, and conquer.

We learned firsthand the value of being surrounded by people who have vision, construct a plan, and take action. We witnessed their unshakable faith even—and hope—while our own lay temporarily buried. Unwavering in their enthusiasm, they kept giving us opportunities to live beyond ourselves.

Thankfully, these same people saw into our situation with a bird's eye view, and tactfully spoke truth regarding the toxic relationships we had allowed to influence our family. Strong mentors like Michael Hockett and Larry Templeton warned us—and then coached us—to put firm boundaries back in place. They helped me walk through forgiveness of others and myself. Friends within our inner circle noted out loud, "I noticed you're not in a healthy place. What do you need to change?"

The saying is true: We are the average of the five people we spend the most time with. Make sure the relationships in your inner circle are life-giving.

Sometimes, it's necessary to open your eyes *just enough* to notice who's going in the direction you want to go. Then, *say yes* when they invite you on the journey. And if they don't notice at first, reach out. Call out. (I'm so preaching to myself here!)

One of my favorite cinematic scenes is toward the end of the movie *A Beautiful Mind* (2001). The movie depicts the true story of John Forbes Nash Jr., a mathematician who suffered from paranoid schizophrenia. After a long journey spent in psychiatric hospitals, he was well enough to return to Princeton University, where he worked as a Senior Research Mathematician.

The scene shows Nash standing in the doorway of his class as students spill out into the large corridor. The students are thanking him as they leave the classroom, and one gal stops to speak with him. But before she says anything, he stops her to ask about the person standing behind him.

"Can you see him?"

She glances at the man standing behind Nash.

"Yeah."

Assured that he's not hallucinating, he says, "Okay. I am always suspicious of new people. Now that I know you're real, who are you, and what can I do for you?"

Once he came to terms with the reality of his mental illness, he entered into what Dr. Henry Cloud calls the Fourth Corner. It is the place where we embrace the reality of our need for connection with others. He writes:

> In the simplest terms, a real connection is one in which you can be your whole self, the real, authentic you, a relationship to which you can bring your heart, mind, soul, and passion. Both parties to the relationship are wholly present, known, understood, and mutually invested. What each truly thinks, feels, believes, fears, and needs can be shared safely.
>
> On the best teams, in business or in war, this is what happens. And in the best lives (2016, 52-53).

. . . And in the best lives. During those seasons when we struggle to find our footing as fear and doubt wreak havoc on our souls, and the courage to stay present and accept reality evades us . . . we can—we *must*—surround ourselves with people who help us stay grounded in reality. People who will live in Corner Four with us.

It's a vulnerable place to be and yet when we isolate, refusing to reach out, we are eventually left "gasping for relational air," as Cloud succinctly portrays it. You know, when I finally decided I wanted to heal from the crazy cycle of the three-corner roundabout, I moved into Corner Four. There, for a time, I rode on the coattails of those around me who were already living legacies built on timeless principles, success habits, and victorious mindsets.

Thankfully, there are mentors and coaches at every level who we can reach out to to help us grow and develop our potential. Chris LoCurto's company, (which I talked about in chapter three), is one such company. Their expertise at guiding people to find the root of what's holding them back and then work through forgiveness and healing and devise a solid strategy to move forward is the reason they are sought out by high-level achievers.

It's exciting to be on a lifelong path of stretching and growing, reaching out to mentors and coaches who are ahead at every turn, who are successfully teaching what they've learned along the way. Who is in your community?

Who might you need to reach out to?

Who are you coaching or mentoring?

Passion diminishes. I know. I was there. *We* were there. And we know what it's like to feel hopeless, like change is out of reach.

Looking back, I'm eternally grateful for the mentors and coaches who were already successful in their marriages and parenting. They were already successful in their leadership, businesses, and communities. All of them had previously navigated hard seasons in their own lives, and through the help of mentors and coaches in *their* lives, their hearts were healed. Equipped and enabled, they generously opened their lives to us, shared their journey and guided *us* toward healing. They helped ensure that the stories we were telling ourselves were based on truths.

As we grew, our storyboard took on different verbiage. I began editing out the shame and control and replaced them with forgiveness and grace. I edited out fear and doubt, applying courage and conviction instead. It took time, but slowly, passion and ambition to serve others began to be restored.

We can decide at any moment to be the person we wanted to be. Like I said earlier, sometimes we lose our way. But my point to all this is, those questions at the beginning of this chapter? *What is life like for you?* And, *where are you at?* Those are the questions we need to ask one another within the communities where we live and work. It's when we open ourselves up to learn within the context of relationships and connection that we can grow. I'll say it again, we can't give what we don't have. Ask successful people what the cornerstone of their success is and they're bound to tell you it's the mentors and coaches in their lives who ask great questions and, like

I mentioned earlier, get them to think about their thinking. To think about the stories we're telling ourselves.

Mentors like Stephen R. Covey via his audio book, and coaches via the parenting class came at exactly the right time when we needed it most. And, instead of "gasping for relational air," we were given the oxygen of a community. Not just any community. A village brimming with energetic action-takers. People who saw our potential and raised the expectation. Mentors who asked tough questions and didn't accept excuses.

Engaging in relationships with authentic, wholehearted, visionary leaders made a tremendous impact on us. Those leaders helped us change our storyline, get out of the rut of complacency, overcome fear and doubt, and get back to living a legacy abounding in hope.

What is life like for you?

Where are you at?

What might it look like if we purpose to live our legacies within the context of deep, meaningful connections?

The Power of Authentic Engagement and Deep Connections

My cousin Cherilee is one of my mentors (though I don't think she realizes it). With every visit, I come away with a wealth of wisdom. A visionary wife and mother of five young boys, she's one of those people whose passion is contagious.

During one visit, she told me a story that demonstrates the kind of vulnerability that cultivates a culture of connection. She related to me how their family filled the front row at their church. I imagined her five squirmy boys, ages one to eight, between her and her husband—the epitomes of patience.

She went on to tell me about the woman who approached her after the service, a grandmotherly type with a soft-spoken voice. How the woman told her about her recent retirement from a career as a teacher and how she had been praying for and seeking a way to serve and love young mothers. She asked my cousin, "Would it be all right if I came to your home once a week to help you with anything you need? I can hold babies, read to them, fold laundry, whatever would be most helpful to you."

Cherilee said yes.

"You know," Cherilee, with faith and hope dancing in her eyes, told me later, "God is faithful. A week after she began helping, our two-year-old broke his femur and was in a body cast. God sees our lives and He goes before us. He knew I'd need the extra help."

I suspect Cherilee—and her husband, Zach—don't realize what a tremendous influence they are to those around them. They live in that place where telling a story splashing over with joy, adventure, faith, growth, deep connections, and passion means cultivating a culture of vulnerability and transparency in which they let people *in*. They model what Dr. Henry Cloud says: "... the capacity to build deep connections comes first of all from *outside* ourselves; then we internalize it neurologically, biologically, psychologically, and otherwise, through good connections, modeling, and the like" (*The Power of the Other*, 2016, 175).

People like Cherilee and Zach love people well because they allow themselves to receive love from the outside first, integrating it into the story of their family. Empathetic, generous, open ... they're Energy Givers who leave others feeling renewed, inspired, and challenged to pursue big dreams. Weaved into the fabric of who they are, they have those attributes to lavish on others.

In fact, writing this book is an example of the power of others in our lives. This last week, I found an old, worn file folder thick with papers. The label reads in large, bold black letters: **"Goals."** Yesterday, sitting at the dining room table with cups of coffee nearby and sunshine streaming through the open window (a rare occasion here in Germany where it's typically overcast), LeRoy and I slowly went through the file. Each of us silently read through the goal sheets and lists of dreams dating back to 1996.

"Hey, look at this." I turned the paper toward my husband. " 'Finish writing book by December 1, 1996.' "

His eyes met mine as he showed me the paper in front of him. " 'Write and publish book. September, 1997.' "

Huh. We continued reading.

" 'Help Sharon finish writing her book. April, 2004.' " In fact, every year, sometimes two or three times during the year, LeRoy or I had made a note regarding my writing and publishing of a book. Discouragement stood watching on the doorstep of my heart. Disappointment leaned provocatively against the gate.

And yet . . .

About a year and a half ago, I attended an online virtual summit hosted by Chandler Bolt of Self-Publishing School. I was blown away by the speakers as they told about their experience of authoring books.

"Every. Single. Person," I told my husband, speaking slowly for emphasis, "said something to the effect of having a writing coach, a team, a mentor, or *someone* to encourage them. Someone who pushed them to stay congruent with their vision. Someone who consistently poured fuel on their passion."

"So, who is your writing coach?" LeRoy asked.

"I mean, I see the value of coaches to achieve goals . . ." Long pause. "Still, I think I can do this on my own." This, in spite of the fact that I work hard to create a culture in which we value relationships and the power of mentors and coaches. I mean, you'd think I've learned my lesson, right? That I'd take my own advice? Another eighteen months, two more summits—and zero progress on the book—went by before I finally humbled myself and admitted, "I need help."

I invested financially to get connected to a whole community of authors and authors-to-be, experienced—published—mentors, and *the best part ever*: a skilled and gifted coach. And finally, *finally*, I allowed relationships to help me overcome limits and achieve my stretch goals.

Step by step, my writing coach has taken me from my scattered ideas (literally all over the board), to completing an outline and finishing a manuscript. Along the way, I experienced moments when I got overwhelmed and wanted to quit. My coach, Ramy, kept infusing me with vision and the next small step toward seeing the vision become reality.

For twenty years, I've stated the goal of writing a book. I could get hung up on that ... or I can humbly learn from it by acknowledging a stubborn prideful streak and then overcoming it by reaching out to others for help.

You know how I mentioned "divine breadcrumbs" earlier? Two nuggets of wisdom I learned the hard way: first, you have ideas to contribute to the world. Something that will make a positive difference. The world needs your unique idea brought in a way that only you can deliver. (I know you know this.) Second, don't wait. What I wish I realized earlier is that *now matters*. Taking action and getting to work on the vision inside you, acts as a conduit to ignite energy—*to fuel passion*. It may not happen as quickly as you hope. Yes, it will require courage and grit ... attributes gleaned from being around mentors and coaches who have been where you are, grown, and are now leaps and bounds ahead of you. And then, consistent actions over time create momentum as we move from where we are in our current narrative to where we want the story to go.

(Do I sound like I'm playing on a continuous loop? Imagine yourself with your hands cupped around your favorite beverage. And me ... earnest eyes and expression, passion and urgency compelling me to go on: *this is your one life here this side of eternity. Don't waste it. Invest it well.*)

Sometimes, we need to take out a notepad and write down a person's dreams as they bravely whisper them to us. Because, sometimes the plotline is wrought with adversity, loss, and pain. Sometimes, the disappointment in ourselves or from others feels too heavy to get back up on our own again. Hopelessness stalks us. In defense, we imagine that passion is the culprit, so we build walls between ourselves and our dreams—and subsequently, we cut off hope. *Better not to dream,* we tell ourselves. *Prevention is better than intervention,* we justify. And that has great application to a lot of areas of life. But not when it comes to leaning into *what could be* if we risk vulnerability in the pursuit of changing our stories and making a difference. Not to mention the healing we can experience when championed by mentors and coaches—by visionary leaders. And in the process, honor the pursuit of something bigger than ourselves.

Rachel Swanson experienced this first hand. On a missions trip to Lodwar, Kenya in 2009, she interacted with the children living in the city's landfill. There she witnessed a group of barefoot children ranging in age from two- to nineteen-years old squatting in a circle as the oldest boy in the group divvied up a can of beans between them. Their feet bore the scars and open wounds from scavenging amongst shards of glass and jagged metal. Later, after returning home in Southern California, she couldn't shake the images . . . and a vision was born. She decided to assemble a team to run a school where the children could live and receive a quality education.

Since 2010, New Hope Children has rescued more than thirty children from the landfills and streets. Their mission is "Serving God by helping to restore the lives of abused, homeless and disadvantaged youth by empowering them with life skills and education." Upon arrival at New Hope, the staff immediately begins to script a new narrative for the children, telling them they're heroes, "because they inspire us daily with their courage, resilience, and positive life choices (http://www.newhopechildren.com/meet-the-children.html)."

A new vocabulary—and vision—for their storyboards: Courage. Resilience. Positive life choices.

Rachel and her team of nineteen board members both in Lodwar and in the United States are working hard to equip New Hope's Heroes with the character, training, and tools to become visionary leaders in their community.

Already one graduate, Nicodemus, the eldest of five siblings, hopes to receive training in the States to learn sustained agriculture in desert climates so he can take his knowledge to help the community in Lodwar. At thirteen-years old he used to feed his five younger brothers by taking the food scraped into a bucket and left underneath a restaurant sink. Then one day, he saw the dish washer spit in the bucket. He says he stopped collecting the scraps because he didn't want to feed it to his brothers. That same year, New Hope brought him to their safe house and his story changed.

While Nicodemus dreams of owning his own recording studio, for now he hopes to learn new ways of producing sustainable food sources. Rachel's legacy of love engages and connects with those who've joined her team, supporters, the young Heroes at New Hope, and an entire city.

The best we can hope for? Whether we're in a season of survival or a season of thriving, it's imperative to immerse ourselves in a community that values change and growth. To get around people who live wholehearted, believe we have more in us than we realize and will help us discover opportunities to grow our potential. Mentors who will raise the expectation and call out the Hero in us. In so doing, we can live a narrative that outlives our lives.

"It may brief well, but how does it execute?" asks my son, Isaiah. He waits while I ponder his question. At first, I'm not sure how to answer. The issue is accountability as his question comes at the end of one of my "brilliant lectures." I'm famous (or infamous?) for my diatribes without an action plan. But then it dawns on me.

"Great question! I'm not exactly sure *how* that executes. Let's brainstorm possible solutions together." I learned through experience (and continue to learn) the execution happens in cultures when they honor risk taking and adventure for the sake of living larger than ourselves. Authentic, wholesome, encouraging, inspiring *connections* which fuel passion, spark ideas, and promote a sense of fortitude for the journey.

Settling for status quo is not a solution. It's not okay to allow our dreams to flatline. We're not the only ones affected by our lives—for better or worse. Someone's breakthrough may be on the other side of our step of faith.

The world does not benefit from us playing small. Our lives have purpose and it's in the moments when we reach out and engage with one another's stories that the world grows smaller and our hearts expand.

Ronna Snyder, popular speaker and author of the book, *Hot Flashes from Heaven*, reveals an epiphany about living our legacies. "Your life leaves behind a fragrance long after you're gone. Make sure it's a sweet one" (2008, 138).

If we want our stories to leave a sweet fragrance long after we're gone, we must embrace our need to connect, to value people and relationships above all else. Some seasons will feel unbearably hard. It will feel vulnerable and scary. Remember, you are not your circumstances.

"What is life like for you?"

It's a simple question.

All those moments when we sit across from another human and ask, "Where are you at?" It doesn't have anything to do with geography. It's a soulful question, meant to dignify the other and their journey. To inspire and cultivate potential.

"Help me understand."

Passionate. Soulful. Engaged. Connected.

Whispers possibility: *And, also . . .*

8. Always Be On a Mission

Men wanted for hazardous journey. Low wages, bitter cold, long hours of complete darkness. Safe return doubtful. Honour and recognition in event of success.
—Ernest Shackleton

Here is a test to find out whether your mission in life is complete. If you're alive, it isn't.
—Lauren Bacall

Every legendary story has its inciting incident. A moment in time where the trajectory of the plotline turns.

Heather Cook's joy is contagious. She radiates hopeful expectancy. Ask her where her joy comes from and her blue eyes gleam as she leans in and says, "Jesus."

And her inciting incident? In the back of a police car during an arrest she knew would send her to prison for the second time.

But like so many legendaries before her, Heather was done with a life riddled with pain and loss.

In her book, *Beyond the Bars*, Heather recounts the night of August 24, 2008. "Everything started to come together. Even in the midst of the fog, I could see so clearly . . . I didn't care how much time I was going to do, I was okay with whatever was in front of me because it was better than what was behind me" (2015, 73). And what was behind her was a life of trafficking, prostitution, mental and physical abuse, along with drug and alcohol addiction. She was the mother of five children, all of them either adopted out or growing up in the foster care system.

With plans to get on a plane the next day to meet a trafficker in New York, something clicked inside her when she saw the police officer's lights in her rearview mirror. Although in the past, she had entertained thoughts of suicide, suddenly the flashing lights on the top of that car ignited hope ... that this time ... the narrative would change.

On a two-hour drive to Stuttgart, Germany, my daughter and I got to hear Heather's story in person.

"I was facing a ten-year prison sentence. And even though I didn't want to be in prison for that long, I had already decided to accept whatever happened next. In fact, I wrote a letter to the judicial system, apologizing for everything in my past and thanking them for their efforts to intervene in my life. On a Wednesday in December, I stood before the judge, waiting for the sentence. When he asked me if there was anything I wanted to say, I asked if I could read the letter and he gave me permission."

About an hour outside of Stuttgart, the traffic is usually heavy and slow-going. Cars merged into our lane as Heather slowed, smiling and waving drivers in.

She continued, "I read the letter and then he explained my sentence. I would spend the next eighteen months in the correctional facility with another five years of probation after that."

She went on to tell us about the women who visited her from a local faith community, about the constant support and love she received, and how they taught her what it looked like to grow in faith. Later, after her release from prison, they continued to mentor her and teach her everyday life skills—something she had never learned.

Heather went on to form a group that reached out to prostitutes. She befriended them, mentored them, and spoke love and value into their lives. When she and her husband received military orders to move, she wanted to do one last thing for them to demonstrate their value.

Paying forward a measure of the grace given her, she took them to a formal, high-end restaurant. "Order anything you want," she said, "You're worth it."

An inciting incident, a moment of truth, the trajectory of a plotline changed. Mentored, loved, valued. An inspirational story of redemption in which the protagonist goes from hopeless to living a legacy of giving hope to others.

I'll never forget the first time I heard the word "injustice." Or, maybe it was the first time it crossed the synapses of my brain and left an impression.

Jeff and Karla are quietly changing the world by simply being who they are. "Lives of valor" is what comes to mind when their name is mentioned.

We spent many, many evenings sitting in their living room engaged in the kinds of conversations that change people. I don't think I ever left one of those exchanges the same as when I arrived. One evening, we got on the topic of "What is your *not-okay?*"

Karla didn't hesitate. "Injustice."

The word, and all it entailed, landed softly in the middle of the room. Injustice? Why had that never occurred to me before?

My mind flashed back to the juvenile detention center I passed during all those walks between the high school and my home. Isn't justice what they doled out to delinquents? All my life, my perception of justice was a person getting what they deserved.

But *in*justice?

The conversation continued. As the focus turned to me, I didn't hesitate either, "Apathy. That's my not okay. That life is so short and people take time for granted. Lack of passion. Lack of drive. Lack of vision."

That dialogue took place in 1998. Fast-forward ten years to the spring of 2008.

Auschwitz-Birkenau Concentration Camp, Poland.

Standing inside the gate at Birkenau, the eerie stillness envelops the vast and wide-open space.

There's a scene in the movie *Schindler's List* (1993) which depicts Oskar Schindler talking to the Jewish people who worked in his factories. World War II has ended. And yet, although he saved over a thousand lives, in the closing scene he's overcome with remorse that he didn't do more. He looks at his car and wonders aloud why he didn't sell it to save ten more. He removes a gold pin from the lapel of his coat, "This is gold. Two more people. They would've given me two more. At least one. They would've given me one. One more. One more person. One more person who's dead . . . for this."

I thought about that scene as I stood on the railroad tracks where thousands arrived daily. They traveled in cattle cars, only to be separated upon their arrival. The women, children, elderly, and sick walked the fifteen-minute walk to the gas chambers and crematorium. Those who appeared strong enough to work were imprisoned in the work camps.

Our family had already walked through Auschwitz. There are no words to describe what it's like to stand in front of a glass case, the contents behind it hundreds of children's shoes. And the moment my seven-year-old's hand clasped in mine as she looked up at me, eyes brimming with tears, and quietly asked, "Mommy? Did they kill all those children?"

Against the advice of the Auschwitz website not to bring children younger than fourteen, we exposed our children, and ourselves, to an intensely painful part of history. To a legacy of hatred. To the atrocities of genocide. Suddenly, injustice became something tangible.

We cried a lot of tears that day. I'm not saying you need to expose yourself or others to the horrors of injustice—in fact, we went against our better judgment and I'd probably advise against exposing your younger children if you asked me. Thankfully, we didn't turn away in an effort to deny the pain. We leaned *into* the pain and used it to solidify our convictions: every person has a right to be treated with honor and dignity . . . and injustice is not only *not okay,* living a legacy of love means fighting for justice. It means being a voice for those whose voice is silenced.

Here's a hard truth: We returned home, my husband went back to work, my children resumed their studies, and I settled back into my routines of managing our home. We paid bills, washed laundry, and completed to-do lists. We laughed with friends over dinners and enjoyed our Friday Family Fun Nights with pizza and a movie. And gradually, the ache of injustices in the world subsided.

It wasn't a bad thing. In fact, I *wanted* my children to return to their raucous play, forays into the forest to explore, and the occasional complaint over an undesirable dinner. I felt more grateful than ever when one of them struggled with an especially difficult school assignment. Tears over Algebraic equations? Yes, this felt *normal.* A relief in light of the new insights we learned about the incomprehensible sufferings in the world.

And isn't this the place where we prefer to live our legacy? Amongst spirited discussions over whose team is best and the game's final score? Around the boardroom table finding ways to improve customer service and increase revenues? In the everyday interactions with our colleagues, our spouse, our community—in the smallest of kindnesses? In the fostering of authentic relationships? I know. Rhetorical, right? Certainly, it's in these normal life moments where we show up, lean in, live, serve, and love. This is healthy.

But somewhere along the way, comfort morphs into complacency. Apathy stokes the coals of selfishness. The inciting incident fades into the background.

It happens in every cultural setting. Whether a top Fortune company, a non-profit organization, a sports team, a marriage, or family, the vision for the story you're narrating, must stay top of mind.

No one is immune to what Bill Hybels, founding and senior pastor of Willow Creek Community Church, in his book on leadership proverbs, calls "a vision leak."

He writes in *Axiom*:

> Some leaders believe that if they fill people's vision buckets all the way to the top one time, those buckets will stay full forever. But the truth is, people's buckets have holes of varying sizes in their bottoms. As a result, vision leaks out.
>
> When you can tell it's time for a vision refill, use every communication means available to you to repaint the picture of the future that fills everybody with passion. And then take it a step further by reporting progress on the vision's achievement. Trust me, when you wrap a little real-life proof around the accomplishment of your [organization's] vision and show that

the dream really is coming true, the fog will start to clear and people's heads will start to nod. "Oh yeah!" they'll suddenly remember. "I get it! I get it! This is what we're about! This is why we exist as an [organization]" (2008, 52).

Nothing riles me like the pervasive sense that our vision is dimming and apathy is setting in. The symptoms usually correspond with "lack," as in, a lack of gratitude, lack of joy, lack of passion, lack of peace.

This is typically when companies hold off-sites for team-building, strategizing, relaxing, and getting clear on the vision again. Coaches give a rallying speech on the field after a particularly unenthusiastic practice. Couples go away on a weekend retreat. And parents call a family meeting.

Sometimes, the problem is a lack of awareness that complacency has crept in and everyone has comfortably settled into status quo. We become travel-weary without ever leaving home. Inertia sets in and we forget the mission and why we were ever on a mission in the first place. Except, we don't have to settle. In fact, we're not designed to settle.

Have you ever heard someone say, "They made a world of difference in my life?" Perhaps you've said it yourself. As visionary leaders, we're called to steward our impact, to make a difference in the world by making a world of difference in those we influence. And, I'm assuming that if you've read this far, you aren't okay with status quo either. That you desire to wake up each day excited to take action, move the mission forward, make a positive impact, and invest in a legacy that outlives your life.

To have the courage to engage in the rising action, climax, falling action, and dénouement. Your overture, entr'acte, and encore.

Time is precious. We can live a better story. Our moments can make a positive impact. But we must live wide awake. Aware of unlimited possibilities. Look for the inciting incident. The twists in the plotline, engaging at every turn.

There are seasons in my life in which I've felt like the noble peasant, Westley, in the movie, *The Princess Bride* (1987). In the scene where he is supposed dead, he is brought to Miracle Max where they lay him on a table and Miracle Max says, "He probably owes you money, huh? I'll ask him."

To this, Inigo Montoya says, "He's dead. He can't talk."

"Woo hoo hoo! Look who knows so much, heh? Well, it just so happens that your friend here is only mostly dead. There's a big difference between mostly dead and all dead. Please, open his mouth."

Taking old bellows, he proceeds to force air into Westley's lungs. He continues, "Now, mostly dead is slightly alive. Neh, all dead . . . well, with all dead, there's usually only one thing that you can do."

Inigo asks, "What's that?"

"Go through his clothes and look for loose change." At this point, Miracle Max removes the bellows and, leaning over Westley, yells, "Hey! Hello in there! Hey, what's so important? What you got here that's worth living for?" He pushes on Westley's abdomen.

"Truuue looove."

Inigo says, " 'True love.' You heard him. You could not ask for a more noble cause than that."

Sure, noble causes abound. After all, we've worked hard to cultivate a culture with core values and vision. We're clipping along, taking the right actions, impacting our world. And then, somewhere along the way, it suddenly feels like we're mostly dead. But the story isn't done.

"What you got here that's worth living for?"

For many years, I collected wake up calls. Most hotels in the United States have, as part of their customer services, a complimentary wake up call. Just dial the front desk and inform them of what time you want the phone in your room to ring and they'll set it so that you receive a phone call at the determined time.

At first, I requested wake up calls for the practical reason—I needed an alarm clock. But then I noticed the various types of calls I received in different hotels. Sometimes I picked up the phone to the automated, robotic recording, "This is your wake up call." *click.* Other times, an actual employee called, the voice a flat, cheerless, "Hello Mrs. Olson. This is your wakeup call," as if annoyed by this part of their job description.

Still other times, I answered the phone to a bright, "Good morning. This is the wakeup call you requested." And the employee actually waited for a response before hanging up, "You're welcome, Mrs. Olson," came the reply to my thank you, "I hope you have a great day."

I even decided on a winner and a runner up. The latter is the personal call from a front desk employee at Grouse Mountain Lodge in Whitefish, Montana. Although I don't remember the specifics, I remember how they caused me to *feel* . . . their enthusiastic voice infusing the day with a sense of excitement and anticipation. And the winner is Edelweiss Resort in Garmisch, Germany. In fact, our family memorized the animated and infectious automated greeting, "Grüss Gott and good morning. It's time to wake up. The world's greatest playground is waiting."

I thought about all the times in my life when I received wake up calls that jolted me from a state of complacency. The death of a loved one. A diagnosis. Disheartening news. And I recalled the wakeup calls we've celebrated . . . news of wedding engagements, births, graduations, milestones, promotions.

Here's my epiphany: *We* can be living, breathing wakeup calls. We can steward a legacy every single day that helps jolt people from a state of complacency and apathy. When we show up for our lives, live on mission, speak life over people and into circumstances, bring our ideas and solutions to problems . . . When we invest in relationships and seek to develop the leader in those around us . . . When we turn challenges into opportunities and lean into both the easy and difficult moments wholehearted, confident, encouraged, with true love as our "what's here that's worth living for," then . . .

We can bring transformation to our communities, organizations, marriages, companies, and parenting endeavors. This is revolutionary. Do you see how our personal healing, growth, and success can be the catalyst for others to heal, grow, and succeed?

The entire trajectory of Heather's life changed when she decided enough was enough. She didn't know *how* to go about changing her story. She didn't know women from a nearby faith community would visit her in prison, build a relationship with her, and mentor her. But here's the thing . . . we don't have to figure out the details before we decide to edit the manuscript of our lives. We don't have to know *how* to create a masterpiece. We simply need to believe it's possible. We have to *want* different words, different scenes, to fill the storyboard. We need to have the courage to accept the reality of what is, be open to possibilities of how we might want to write the following scenes, and then *move* in that direction.

In his book, *The Happiness of Pursuit*, Chris Guillebeau writes, "The rule of improv theater is to always keep the story going. You finish your part and ask, 'And then?' The idea is that every story can be extended, sometimes with unexpected results." (2014, 54)

". . . Any given moment can change your life. For some people it's a conversation that opens the doors of possibility: a new business opportunity, perhaps, or a new relationship. For others it's the sudden shift in perspective: *I don't have to live like this anymore.*" (2014, 55)

"Any given moment . . ."

Fast-forward another year to 2009.

A dozen women planned to go away on a weekend scrapbooking retreat. The event would take place in an old family-owned winery, which doubled as a bed and breakfast inn on the banks of the Mosel River in Bernkastel-Kues, Germany. During the weeks leading up to the anticipated getaway, a sort of buzz, palpable and provocative, permeated their conversations. It almost made me want to take up scrapbooking just so that I could join them for the weekend. Almost.

(I, too, scrapbooked at one time, only to discover I don't love it.)

Finally, one day a couple of weeks before the retreat, I pulled my friend, Dani, who was coordinating the whole thing, aside. "Dani," I tried not to sound needy, "you know I don't scrapbook, but can I come along on the retreat, bring my books, and read during the weekend?"

She laughed, "Of course!"

Little did I know how that weekend would set not just me, but our entire family, on a path that would find us standing in a tiny ramshackle building, conversing with teachers, in the African bush. From a paradigm-altering conversation in the home of Jeff and Karla, to that moment ten years later in Auschwitz-Birkenau Concentration Camp where the depth of injustice was made tangible, a single book was about to be my wakeup call, shaking me from my comfort zone.

We arrived at the bed and breakfast, checked in, and deposited our bags in our rooms. The agenda set forth was to have everyone gather their scrapbooking accessories and hordes of photos and meet in the large family room. I took my book, found a nook where I didn't take up room at a table, and began reading *Dangerous Surrender* by Kay Warren.

At the end of the first chapter—which riveted my attention—Warren writes out a prayer. I paused extra long on one sentence in particular, "Forgive me for my complacency, my apathy, my ignorance" (2007, 35).

She writes about her visit to Rwanda. Of visiting the Rwandan genocide memorial sites and hearing the personal stories of survivors.

She tells about her experience in a leprosarium in the Philippines. How she learned the gift of presence is more meaningful than any material gift.

She shares the story of her visit with prostitutes in Kolkata, India. That moment when she naïvely "asked them how they remained joyful in such [horrendous] circumstances.

"Tears spilled onto their lovely faces. 'Joy? My joy ended the minute I came here from my village,' said one. 'There is no joy.' We sat in silence for a few moments trying to absorb the horror of their lives. I couldn't stop myself from asking the obvious question: 'Why don't you leave? Why don't you just stop being a prostitute?' They replied as one: 'What would we do? We have no skills. How would we live? Our families are expecting the money we earn. There is no escape' " (2007, 166).

I spent the weekend sobbing hot tears that drenched my cheeks and dripped off the end of my nose. I kept hiding in my room to read because of the torrent of emotion that turned my vision blurry and my face a mess. I read straight through the entire book, tissues piled next to me on the bed.

When I arrived home, my family greeted me and, the six of us in the dining room, my husband asked about my weekend. A rush of tears bubbled to the surface as my family sat there, wide-eyed. Stunned. Trying to answer while simultaneously pulling it together, I half-spoke, half-sobbed a guttural, "We need to go to Africa."

Africa? I honestly hadn't even processed that far. At least, not consciously. Yet, there I stood, my reckless declaration settling around us as we all stared at one another speechless.

(Here's the thing about my husband: he's brilliant at executing on a vision. Africa? He made an action plan and set it in motion. I'm telling you, it takes a team, community, village . . .)

And that's how we ended up visiting our friends, Bob and Amy, in Africa seven months later. Me, naïvely asking questions out of context.

The experience changed our family's story. Serving at the nearby orphanage meant letting ourselves in the front door, removing our shoes, and rubbing some disinfectant on our hands. We arrived at lunchtime which meant there were four women attempting to feed fifteen babies all under the age of two. The six of us were a welcome sight indeed.

Out in the bush, we played games with the children in the village. LeRoy and I taught a couple of marriage workshops, (which I'm certain our friend, Ron, graciously changed the interpretation whenever we made an irrelevant, out of context remark).

We were welcomed wherever we showed up. "Red tape" protocols and bureaucracies didn't exist. It emboldened us. In Africa, it really does take a village to achieve pretty much anything. Count yourself in. Step up and be helpful in the moment.

We lived the saying, *see a need, fill a need*, in real-time. The needs and immediacy of initiative allowed us to experience a level of servant leadership we hadn't known before. Fear dissipated as we realized no one worried if we "did it wrong" . . . the smallest acts of service were helpful.

Yet, I wrestled internally for a long time after returning home. I grappled with the question of why I got to live a life of comfort and ease and abundance while entire nations were experiencing civil wars, hunger, and disease. What about the thousands of orphans? How was I supposed to fight injustices of this magnitude?

It's easy to slip into an extreme, either punishing oneself and choosing deprivation in the name of justice, or numbing oneself, shrugging it off as *well, I'm just one person, what can I do?*

Stay present. Listen to your heart.

Pay attention to the unfolding story right where you are. The overture, entr'acte, and encore. What is the context of your story? What comes bubbling to the surface of your life at the moments of rising action, climax, falling action, and dénouement? "What you got here that's worth living for?"

The journey to Africa, (and all our travels to foreign countries), has opened up our world. It's given us perspective and caused us to be more aware—to see people and to love bigger right where we are.

Of course, mostly, our days exist as extraordinary in the ordinary, don't they? The inciting incidents subtle and almost unnoticeable to the untrained eye.

Bethany and Craig are quiet revolutionaries. Being in their presence is like stepping into a story filled with adventure and imagination. While there're plenty of misadventures, too—with seven children, newborn up to eleven years old, there's bound to be—they are creating a culture which values lifelong learning and solution-oriented thinking.

They live in the rich context of relationships that care for and watch over one another. And Bethany captures their unfolding story with camera in hand and the words on her blog, lyrical and poetic, even when describing the toddler's latest fiasco in attempting to flush a toy down the toilet.

Bethany is cultivating a generous culture of language and music and art. She plays the piano. She's a painter. A poet. A storyteller—not just reading the words written by someone else, but she is commandeering a narrative in which her family experiences life as both an exciting enterprise as well as a full-bodied consonance—the rhythm and cadence of their routines making room for the resolution of all the various notes.

I asked Bethany whether she enjoys change or routine more. She smiled resolute, "Routine. I don't like change."

The thing to remember is that while principles are nonnegotiable and values are constant, our stories are dynamic. Fluid. They're in perpetual motion.

So, how does someone who doesn't like change, live into the reality of dynamic stories? Bethany brilliantly nurtures a vision for creativity and spontaneity within structures of order.

As my editor, Spencer, pointed out, "Pianissimo is only really soft if it is heard next to fortissimo."

Bethany is also a runner whose route and distance never vary. Except for the obvious seasons like when expecting a baby, she's run the same 3.9 miles on the same route for the last ten years.

Her running routine is symbolic of the nonnegotiables in their home: their core values passed down from her and her husband to the oldest and each successive child. There is a profound sense of security, strength, and confidence in their home.

And this is the challenge for all of us. To be self-aware. To know our strengths and to build on them because this is when the trajectory of our lives changes. Confident in who we are, and what our core values are, we're able to identify our "not okay." The noble cause that is our "What you got here that's worth living for?" To be willing to change our story to make sure it's authentically ours, so we can effectively impact our world. Bethany is the one who taught me to "Step a little closer. Stand a little taller." To live undaunted.

Identifying what keeps us up at night and gets us out of bed in the morning sets us on a course to put our stake in the ground, and helps us prevent vision leaks. And all within the context of our unique story dynamics.

Bethany's home is a fluid, dynamic mixture of beauty and art and creation and story-telling (both figuratively and tangibly), because all this motion occurs as the fortissimo within the quiet structure and routines of her pianissimo.

Sometimes the story we're telling is more like an impressionist's painting. Historically, the Impressionist painters were spurned. The era of the day valued straightforward lines. Impressionistic paintings depict motion.

How many times I absorb myself in capturing the moment on camera, zooming in and out, careful to take out the blur, when someone exclaims nearby, "Wow! Did you see that? Now that was awesome!" How many times I've mumbled to myself, *No. I was busy trying to get a perfect picture.*

This concept has also reached into the creation of this book. It takes an enormous amount of faith to commit to writing while my family continues to live dynamically around me. I'm afraid I'll miss something. That I'll miss the epiphanies and laughter and growth moments I'm accustomed to in the culture of our family. That I'll miss what's in motion.

Yet my concerns are proving to be unfounded. Even during focused writing, my children wander in, sit in the reclining chair nearby, and say, "Mom? Can I talk to you?" And what I was so afraid of, that I would either miss out on the story going on around me or that I couldn't be "disturbed," is instead creating a scene I didn't expect. They seek me out to invite me into their story.

As for refocusing on the writing at hand? Ah! The grace! I pick up right where I left off. Though when I return to the project, I'm richer for having engaged in the stories in motion. (Sometimes, they even give me a golden nugget to insert into the writing at hand!)

And there it is. The telling of a dynamic story. To engage in the rising action within the rising action. Is that even possible? Perhaps.

"Expose your kids to as many experiences as possible," Penny told me.

As Penny was one of my mentors, I listened to and internalized her counsel.

"Take them places. Take them to the library, to live theater, to the park, to friends' houses, even simply walk around downtown and finish with an ice cream cone. And talk to them about the experiences. Ask them, 'What if?' Encourage them to imagine."

So, I did. The practice of rules, structure and pianissimo set within the fluidity, improvisation and fortissimo of our moments throughout our day. To be open to how the trajectory of the story might unfold.

Ah, to architect culture around the (terrifying) romance and adventure of possibilities. To stay open and aware of how we might be helpful. The mission might look like mentoring inmates in prison, righting injustices, battling complacency and challenging the status quo. It may be starting a business, a neighborhood book club, or serving sandwiches to those who are homeless. Perhaps it's the mission to adopt or do foster care. Maybe it's holding orphans in a far-off place or maybe it's curling up on the couch with your five-year-old to read a book.

How might we become visionary leaders by staying open to the idea that any given moment could change our life? That what we got here that's worth living for is true love.

That there are as many ways to fulfill the mission of loving big as there are human beings in the world and all we have to do is allow the narrative to be fluid, in motion, Impressionistic ... the fortissimo against the backdrop of pianissimo.

9. Transformational and Empowering Leadership

You can't live a perfect day without doing something for someone who will never be able to repay you.
—John Wooden

Transformational Leadership

It happened again. I commented to a mom about the character qualities I saw in her children and told her well done, only to receive the downward glance and dismissive nod of the head.

"I don't think I've been a good parent," she said.

By what measure? How do you gauge whether you're a good leader or a bad leader? What if it isn't so cut and dry as the numbers at the end of the fiscal year? Or how many people were in attendance? Or any number of ways we draw conclusions of success or failure based on concrete data?

A few years ago, I stepped off a ten-hour flight into the Fort Lauderdale airport and wound my way through international customs. After retrieving my baggage and passing through all the usual customs booths, I turned down a long hallway toward the terminal. Up ahead, I saw one more booth, a tall, muscular guard standing behind the glass shield. I handed him my passport.

"Where do you live?"

"I live in Germany, sir."

He studied the photo, glancing at me, then back at the photo. He flipped through the pages of the passport. "What are you doing here in Florida?" His deep voice and strong posture commanded respect.

"Attending a conference."

"What do you do?" A slight pause. "Your career?"

I smiled. Rolling my shoulders back a little more, I said, "I'm a full-time homemaker."

Then that man asked me the best question I've ever been asked regarding my industry.

"Are you any good at it?"

In reality, I suppose he asked every traveler the exact same questions. Yet no one had ever asked me if I'm any good at . . . *what*? Making peanut butter and jelly sandwiches? Running our Human Resources department? Being Chief Operating Officer? Corporate project management on everything from potty training to life coaching through an adolescent relationship crisis? I pondered it for several long seconds. I took my time. After all, there wasn't anyone standing in line behind me at the moment. Besides, I wanted to let the moment, and the question, bathe my soul in wonder.

To be a visionary leader, intent on developing people who find possibility and amazement wherever they are, with whomever they interact . . . To invest in relationships so people are empowered to use their strengths and creativity, to take risks, and build wholehearted companies, communities, and families who make a positive difference in the world . . . And in turn, pass the torch. Did this man know the sacred nature of the question he asked? Neither one of us moved as he waited patiently for me to answer.

Finally, I smiled and, tilting my head to the side, said, "Great question! Sometimes. I think if you asked my children, they would tell you that some days are successful and other days we learn a lot about how to improve the story we're living."

He smiled slightly and nodded. "Good."

I reached for my passport and gathered my bags as I continued down the long, wide corridor.

Deep in thought, I walked slowly, reflecting. That question, "Are you any good at it?" played on a continuous loop in my head. At that point, I had poured nineteen years into my life's work, and in my recollection, had never been asked if I was any good at what I did.

My mind flashed back to something my Mother-in-Love had said to me when I had our first baby. "You know, parenting is such a sensitive topic. No parent wants critiques or unsolicited advice. Because it's so personal, it's hard to hear feedback."

I remember her words finding their way into my soul, searching for a place to land. But I think they've flitted around from place to place, never taking root, the desperate longing of my soul for more wisdom, more counsel, a constant disturbance to complacency.

I used to receive affirmations about my parenting with the same downward glance and self-deprecating tone. This seems to be a common response.

Then I had an epiphany. Would the president of a successful corporation answer the same way?

According to Jim Collins, the executive leaders of companies that went from good to great all responded to accolades with the same humble, *It took all of us. We couldn't have achieved all that we did if it hadn't been for the people who work here.*

As I type this, my children have been asked to speak to our faith community on the importance of passing on to the next generation our "Ebenezer" stories. Ebenezer is a reference to the memory of God's faithfulness to the Israelites, recorded in 1 Samuel. Our successes and victories are due to the plethora of leaders who invested deeply into our family, both our marriage as well as parenting. Mentors, coaches, counselors, teachers . . . it would fill a book to recount all the people who have spoken into our lives, sharing their insights and wisdom. Telling us their stories. Challenging us to grow. Pushing us past our comfort zones and inviting us to do things we wouldn't have thought possible.

We wanted to tell a story of love through the culture of our family—thanks to being surrounded by and poured into by a long (extremely long) list of people who exemplify love, we have this ridiculous privilege of being on this journey. What is the vision you're leading? How do you and the people in your company, organization, and family answer, "Are you who you dreamed of being? Is this the vision you had for your life?"

Is the theme clear? Does everyone have a vocabulary for ambition? Do you and the people you're impacting know *how it works here*? What you're about?

Do you value mentors, coaches, and teachers? And, does everyone know they're in a culture that invites feedback and thrives on growth?

So, this question: are you any good at it? At living a narrative that's making a positive impact? At leading with humility, grace, and a vision for the possibility and potential in yourself and in others? At developing the leader in those in your sphere of influence?

There's no hard data to measure. We've held to the perspective, *Did we invest in what we can take with us?*

For us, that means creating a culture where love is expressed through conversations, traveling, experiencing day-to-day life as an art form, cultivating wonder, and serving others. It means investing time to *learn* one another's preferences and practicing generosity.

It means the children spending an exorbitant amount of time working on projects requiring ingenuity, problem solving, utilizing ambitious and service-oriented vocabulary, implementing ideas and practicing followership and leadership.

The boardroom looks different depending on where you are. Leaders must steward the responsibility and privilege to direct action-packed stories with scenes full of impact, vision, and love. Of course, backdrops vary from villages in the African bush to corporate high-rises in the city to dining room tables in homes. But the mission remains the same.

It's up to us to create a culture of honor in our workplaces. To develop cultures of candor and trust.

(Remember what I mentioned earlier on how fun it'd be to have an actual consulting company come assess your family's "bottom line" and help create a team strategy? What might that look like?)

In our family, we use a scale system to gauge strengths and preferences. For instance, regarding preferences, we might say, "On a scale of one to ten, one being *I really don't want to talk in front of a crowd of people* and ten being *I'd love to*, where are you?"

Regarding strengths, it sounds like, "On a scale of one to ten, one being *Focus and follow-through are a growth area in my life* and ten being *I'm excellent at staying focused and following through*, where are you?"

When it comes to leadership, we're constantly gauging ourselves and holding one another accountable. There's a whole list of leadership qualities we value, like listening, empathy, perspective, compassion, and grace.

Are we any good at it? Some moments we're good at employing a heart that listens and empathizes. Other moments we're great. And sometimes we fail. It's a continual practice—a habit, really—to extend grace and forgiveness to one another, believe the best, offer encouragement, things like "Remember who you are."

We're not perfect. We're practicing presence—the deep breath, choosing words laden with blessing and strength. We don't always get it right. And we know this is a safe place to get it wrong, be loved in the midst, and try again.

When the guard asked me if I was any good at being a homemaker, it sent me into deep introspection. *I don't know*, I thought. *Am I?*

Pondering the question has brought me to the conclusion that *we* make a great team. That this isn't about one person's efforts. That if it weren't for the input, critiques, advice, and feedback of an entire (massive) community, we wouldn't enjoy the close relationships and pursue the values and principles that we do today.

Through mountains of books, countless conversations, workshops, conferences, seminars, and faith-based sermons, we continue to soak up knowledge and learn to discern wisdom. Through failures and setbacks, successes and breakthroughs, we are discovering the beauty of embracing the process—the improvisation. Of slowing down. Of breathing deeply in the sacred pauses. To live this adventure.

Perhaps the question that precedes if we're any good at something is if we're doing something that matters. In the culture of our family, people development is paramount. What does your workplace, organization, marriage, church, corporation stand for? It's interesting how many leadership training centers and schools are developed within companies which stand for excellence in service.

What might it look like if we had the mindset that our marriages and our families are leadership training and development centers?

In fact, when our youngest was still an infant and our oldest was six years old, we read the book *The 21 Irrefutable Laws of Leadership*, by John Maxwell (1998), together. In it, Maxwell tells the story about his parents paying him to read good books. Since he and his siblings all grew up to carry on their family's legacy of loving and serving others, I figured we'd integrate this system into our family, too. (This was the only incentive plan we implemented in our family. Well, this and the one dollar for character affirmations that we implemented later. Although we tried an allowance system a couple of times, we found it didn't fit our family's culture of building teamwork and a heart of service.) To this day, I'll pull a book from our shelves and, upon opening it, find a sticky note on the inside cover with a date and a dollar amount stating the agreed upon payment upon completion.

Speaking of books, I learned to not only read deeply, but broadly. While I devoured lessons on leadership, I also read books written by surgeons on the practice of medicine, biographies of other adventurers, parenting books, corporate blogs, and books on mentoring and coaching. Books on business and finance, health and wellness, marriage, and a plethora of books on how to connect more deeply, more intimately, more authentically.

Because, the truth is, I'm not any good at what I do if I'm busy checking off boxes and attending to whatever society deems urgent.

I know I *must* be intentional about building a team of people who care about developing themselves and others.

As leaders, don't we all set out to build a team culture which values investing deeply into the relationships right in front of us, of serving and loving those in our community? Of loving by way of listening? Are we any good at it? We'll keep practicing.

What do we use to measure success? A culture that demonstrates empathy. A team that gives preference to one another. A company, classroom, community that gives generously from their time and other resources. Success means learning and using a vocabulary for "ambition" and then teaching that vocabulary to the people in our organization.

Regarding personal and leadership development, Kelsey Humphreys, author, speaker, and coach, says, "Research it, write it, live it . . . coach it!" It's imperative for us to consider that those we impact, want and *need* the servant leadership we're called to bring to our organizations.

We can learn to lead with wisdom and humility. And we must. We need to step up and lead by example. In our company (which, by now you know I'm referring to our family), we created a culture modeled after corporate training centers and leadership schools. Being a person of faith, I also refer to this as discipleship. Are our people always enthusiastic about diving deep into what it means to lead themselves, cultivate a servant's heart, and look for ways to love bigger? No. But it's the way it works here and the best we can hope is that we'll build a culture where intimacy and deep connections are nurtured in relationships. And out of that, they'll develop their character so they abound in hope, empowered to live a better story, impact their world, and be visionary leaders.

Those who lead with excellence humble themselves and reach out to others for counsel, mentoring, coaching, and honest feedback. We can't un-know stuff. And to selfishly hoard the education and insights we've gleaned in the living of our stories is . . . apathetic. That might sound harsh. But our world is suffering from a wide gap in service-minded, wholehearted leadership. Instead of averting our eyes and nodding timidly, it's time we acknowledge that we can do a lot better when we surround ourselves with trusted counselors who have our backs, implement what they teach us, and then give others the tools and insights to live a more fulfilling legacy. Of course, we don't always have the answers, and sometimes we do it wrong. But, remember, failure isn't fatal and we can learn to value the fact that failure can teach us more than success.

The Power of Empowerment

"When are you the most effective as a leader?"

This is the question I posed to my "board" during this morning's family meeting. One by one, they answered. And all their answers declared one common denominator (in their own personality and style, of course).

Eli: When I'm hanging out with people.

Isaiah: When I'm being pushed out of my comfort zone and being challenged along with others.

Ezekiel: When I'm making a difference in someone's life.

Israel: When I'm helping someone develop their full potential.

Yes, their responses reflect the vision of the culture they grew up in. However, they are most effective leading when they invest in the development of others in a way that honors their unique temperament and strengths.

Bill Hybels talks about this in his book *Courageous Leadership* (2002). He tells the story of the times when he and his team went on leadership retreats and he asked them this exact question. While he acknowledges there are many right answers, in the end it all boils down to how well you invest in leaders to mentor and train them.

Who has mentored you to become a more effective leader? How are you investing in people to develop their best version of themselves … to contribute their servant-leadership more effectively?

We're created for this. This finding of ways to solve problems and make life better, happier, more engaging.

It doesn't matter who you are when you pull into the semi-circle in front of the Coeur d'Alene Hotel and Resort. Everyone is treated like royalty.

My husband and I pulled up in our mini-van for a long overdue and much needed get-away, just the two of us. As in, leaving the four young adults, ages thirteen to nineteen, at home.

As soon as we drove up to the front of the grand entrance, three professionally dressed young men sprang into action. The bellhop pushed a brass luggage carrier in our direction. A valet walked quickly around to the driver's side, greeting my husband as he stepped out.

Once the bellhop loaded our bags from the trunk onto the carrier, he smiled and said, "Right this way, Mr. and Mrs. Olson."

It was as though the valets were quizzed on pictures of arriving guests so they could be greeted by name. Or perhaps, he'd exchanged pleasantries with my husband while I was busy gathering my things from the front seat? Turns out, he did. LeRoy handed the keys to the valet as we turned to follow the young man into the lobby.

As we approached the door, a fair-skinned lad with a frenzy of reddish curls on his head stood at the entrance, his smile and ushering gesture accompanying a cheery, "Welcome to the Coeur d'Alene Resort."

Even the doorman greeted us, I thought.

We followed our bellhop to the check-in, where a woman, who appeared middle-aged, greeted us from behind the counter. LeRoy gave her our name as she checked the registry. I smiled awkwardly at the bellhop and he bowed slightly, saying he'd be nearby and to let him know when we were ready to go to our room, adding that he'd assist.

I would have felt like an imposter in my jeans and bulky hoody if it hadn't been for the fact that they didn't seem to notice what we were wearing. Or driving. Or the fact that we had Samsonite luggage as opposed to Luis Vuitton.

They engaged us with their warm expressions and eye contact. And since I arrived just in time for the spa appointment LeRoy made for me, I kissed him and headed in the direction of The Spa, so glamorous it needed no other name, and awarded MSNBC's "The World's Most Romantic Spa."

Two women greeted me as though they had anticipated my arrival all day. Handing me a menu, they told me to go ahead and order a lunch for two, that it was included in the package my husband scheduled. I walked up a staircase with water cascading down the wall, the soothing splash and gurgle as it landed on the river rocks below an invitation to relax.

Every second of our entire stay (no, that's not an exaggeration or me being dramatic; yes, it's absolutely true) was sheer extravagance and luxury. The staff, from the top management to the wait staff, treated us like royalty. In fact, I noticed they treated everyone like royalty.

Duane Hagadone, owner and CEO of the Coeur d'Alene Resort, has built an empire around the guiding principles of service and leadership. He is known for "seeing the potential in people," and several employees shared their experience of coming in at the lowest job possible, being recognized by Hagadone, and receiving an opportunity to train for bigger leadership roles.

One of the highlights (it's hard to narrow it down!) was the privilege and honor of visiting with the Assistant General Manager, Larry Holstein. He began as a busboy in the original restaurant, Cloud 9, and has been at the resort for forty-eight years. When asked what his favorite part of working there was, he said it was the opportunity to come alongside and mentor others in the service and hospitality industry.

Hagadone's great secret, the success of his luxurious and profitable hotel, was simply that his employees knew they would be recognized and promoted for their hard work and dedication. His employees felt empowered and invested in the story he wanted his guests to experience.

But it doesn't end there with recognition and promotion. Hagadone's legacy is built into the mentoring and coaching culture he's created amongst the staff. Appreciated and cared for, they're inclined to want to turn around and lend a hand to their successor. What if we were all mindful of creating such cultures?

A while back, I asked our children if they felt they were empowered to make meaningful contributions to our team.

"You mean, besides chores?" they answered. Several long seconds passed. Then: "No, not really."

Ah! Excellent feedback. Brutal, yes. Excellent nevertheless. And really, what am I going to do with the wealth of information I just received? Remember, we can't un-know stuff. And this trust—this call to servant leadership, to equip, empower, and release people to go both higher and deeper—that is the core of it all.

This quest for taking mediocre, complacent . . . apathetic cultures and transforming them into vibrant, passionate, empathetic cultures is at the heart of my mission. Since receiving feedback from my people, I've dug deeper, asked more questions, and invested in becoming a leader who finds ways to more effectively develop the leadership in each of the people who live in our home. For you, that may mean your employees, students, colleagues, or those in your community.

"Why are you this way?" and "Are you any good at it?"

Perhaps we need to ask each other these questions more often. Who are your heroes? Who are your mentors? Who has believed in you and called out the greatness in you?

For Bob Goff, author of *Love Does* (2012), it was Randy, his Young Life leader who spontaneously jumped in the car and traveled to Yosemite National Park with Bob. "I'm with you," he said, when Bob told him his plans to live and work in Yosemite, even though he hadn't finished high school yet. It didn't work out for Bob and he returned to high school. But Bob never forgot what it feels like to know that someone has your back. That they're *with you*.

Horst Schultze, Ritz-Carlton Hotel co-founder and revolutionary leader, attends the orientation meeting for new employees. He stands in front of them and tells them what they already know—that he's an important man in the company. But then, he surprises them. He goes on to tell them that if he doesn't show up at the hotel the next day, no one will notice. No one will mind. He pauses to let that truth take hold before emphasizing *their* importance in the company. He reminds them that their colleagues and the hotel customers are *counting on them*. That without their presence, the business and their customers suffer. That their absence is noticed and *felt*.

He pauses again. Then, he looks around the room, slowly meeting their eyes, and asks, "Now, you tell me, out of the two of us, who is most important?"

Schultze has built a world-class customer experience because of the way he empowers his employees. For example, one policy states that every employee has a two-thousand dollar fund to use at their discretion in order to help serve customers. An illustration Schultze relates is that of a customer who tells the waiter in the restaurant the next morning that the television in his room isn't working. The employee takes ownership of the problem, apologizes for the inconvenience, and tells the customer that he'll not only correct the issue himself, but he'll pick up the breakfast tab.

The employee then takes on the responsibility of seeing that the television is repaired or replaced by the time the client returns to his room. He doesn't need to pass it through a chain of command or get approval. The culture creates an environment where employees are expected to problem solve and make decisions. He is the way he is because leadership equips and empowers him to do his work with excellence.

In *The New Gold Standard,* author Joseph A. Michelli, writes, "In the culture of Ritz-Carlton, which emphasizes Service Values like 'I am empowered to create unique, memorable, and personal experiences for our guests' and 'I own and immediately resolve guest problems,' the choice to shift responsibility to someone else is not an option. (2008, 110)"

He goes on, "Service breakdowns will occur in all businesses that are vulnerable to the inevitable shortcomings of humans. But trusting environments encourage staff to quickly circumvent blame and move constructively in the direction of problem resolution. (2008, 111)"

There's the Young Entrepreneurs Across America, whose mission is to mentor college students in entrepreneurship through their training and development program. Through the real-time experience of running their own painting "company" (a team of five or six painters), at Student Painters they learn invaluable lessons that are nearly impossible to learn from textbooks or the classroom. Employee motivation, profitability analysis, and time management are just a few of the skills the students learn.

Jan Martinez, author of *Christ Kitchen* (2013) and founder of the organization by the same name, is empowering women "on the outskirts of society." Christ Kitchen is a non-profit microenterprise helping women overcome "poverty, hopelessness, and the cycle of abuse." Through relationship-building, Jan and her team are mentoring women in everyday life skills as well as training them in job and business skills. Their mission is founded on the faith that no one is beyond God's transforming love and grace and kindness.

Working at a non-profit health clinic in the city of Spokane, Washington, exposed her to the same kinds of, (and in some ways, worse), brokenness she had seen during missionary work in places like Nepal, Viet Nam, and Kenya. While counseling with women, she noticed the deeper issue of a lack of mentorship and support systems to sustain deep, lasting life change. Poverty is far more than an economic standing. It is a lack of resources in any or a combination of physical, emotional, spiritual, or mental resources. Like so many others throughout these pages, she listened to her heart and sought a solution.

She needed something simple and scalable. The answer came in the form of gourmet food mixes. Every Thursday, she draws women in by offering wages combined with the opportunity to be mentored and find healthy, authentic connections.

In her book, *Christ Kitchen*, Jan writes, "Discipleship occurs on every level of the organization from the simplest task to long-range planning. Our little business of selling beans provides the atmosphere for God to do his big business of saving lives.

". . . Quite frankly, one beneficial side effect to this coupling of multi-layers of mentors and mentoring is that the volunteers grow as much as those they serve. The Lord has inspired the development of a community of women at Christ Kitchen—those from the street and from local churches—who are transcending barriers of class, race, and opportunity to form meaningful, faithful relationships which aid mutual maturity." (2013, 44)

Your unique contribution right where you are might be the inspiration, motivation, tipping point, or catalyst to making an impact that outlives your life. Jan's bold, audacious, and unwavering faith and love transcended the stereotypes of the impoverished, calling out the potential in those she serves and leads.

She's created a culture where encouragement, worthiness, and vision are spoken. The message is clear, *you are worthy of love, you have dignity, you are enough.* Their narratives are being re-storied with a vocabulary for ambition—for hope. As a result, stories once filled with heartache and day-to-day survival are being transformed into stories that thrive with impact and hope.

Rory Vaden, author of *Take the Stairs* (2012), tells about his experience of being trained and mentored at the Southwestern Company. Their website says, "We build people. And those people are building great companies." On page twenty in the introduction of Vaden's book, he writes:

> Emotionally spent, and feeling desolate, I sat down on a curb. I'll never forget looking down at my handwritten map and seeing the words "Buckingham Lane" and "Coral Court" merge together by a stream of my running tears.
>
> How did I end up here? Why am I sitting on a curb in Montgomery, Alabama? What was I thinking to get myself into this? Is this really happening to me right now? How am I ever going to survive ninety more days of this?

He goes on to tell about the incomparable training in leadership and development he received during his summers working for their company. Their website reads, "The Southwestern Advantage mission is: to be the best organization in the world at helping young people develop the skills and character they need to achieve their goals."

I've had many, many curbside moments in my life. I suspect you've had a few yourself. Those are the moments in which, if we'll get up, push through, and refuse to quit, then we grow stronger in character. The experience endows us with gifts: we come away a little more equipped, a little more empowered. Wiser. More hopeful. More humble.

And all that abundance? Ah! Then we connect with others and find ways to pass on what we've received.

Why are you this way? Who's challenged you to raise your standards? Who's invested in you, affirmed you're already enough, and at the same time, called out the genius inside of you? In what culture of honor and excellence did the leaders *expect* you to be *a terrific two*? Who empowered you to take action, love bigger, serve bolder, and be visionary?

And in what areas of your life are you passing that torch?

Equip. Empower. Release.

What if we looked for and encouraged the potential in people? As in, what if we assessed all that's been given to us and invested it multi-generationally? What if we did it because it's currency that we get to spend on what we can take with us into eternity?

A couple of months ago, our two oldest started a business, Hybrid Fitness, a training program whose mission is to develop the whole person: body, mind, and spirit.

Within a week, a friend gave them a substantial amount of seed money. "I believe their business is going to have far-reaching impact," said their angel investor.

The next week another friend signed up as their first paying client. "I have forty days to get ready for the PT test," he said. Six days a week at six o'clock in the morning, our friend is valiantly showing up and pushing himself through intense, custom-designed workouts. "For one hour every day," he tells me, "I hate those boys." They laugh and high-five as sweat drips off their chins.

"Transformational" and "empowering" are dynamic concepts in our stories. Let's add them to our list of vocabulary for ambition, and practice them wherever we are, making them a part of the cultures where we live and work.

"Are you any good at it?" Some things transcend hard metrics. While our world grows increasingly more complex and sophisticated at measuring data and statistics, intangibles like relationships, vulnerability, transparency, intimacy, and connection is still inspired by empathy and authenticity. How do we measure transformation and empowerment? The only way I know is to keep living in the context of community and the plethora of stories. There are hundreds of stories I could have added to this chapter. It was a challenge to narrow it to the ones I mentioned. As I said earlier, there is no end to the brilliance in people. The ideas, the art, the solutions.

Right now, today, is the time to live a legacy abounding in hope. To step up and play all in. To make our lives legendary ... the stories that will one day read: *they thought multi-generationally, loved big, and planted seeds that continue to bear fruit.*

Conclusion

You know what it's like to walk into a place where the atmosphere is charged with enthusiasm? Where the employees stand tall, smile, and their greeting is as though they're genuinely glad to see you? Not because you're going to join their club or purchase from their store or from anything else they might get from you. It's just one of those places where you walk in and you know: people are creative here, they are productive, happy, secure. They're having fun and doing work that matters.

I want to be a part of this.

The other day, I researched the average cost per year to attend an Ivy League college. On average, it's about $53,000 per year for tuition, room and board to attend schools such as Harvard, Stanford, or Princeton University.

This got me thinking. For several days. What if I wrote a check to a company for the amount of $212,000—the price of a four-year Ivy League education—to train my child for one year in leadership and entrepreneurship? How might it affect the trajectory of their life to train directly alongside a community who are already far ahead in the work my child wants to do? People who have a track record of success in relationships, business, money, and time. A company with a reputation for being leading learners, humbly reaching out to coaches for accountability themselves. A group of mentors who would teach my grown child the proverbial ropes, "Look, here's what we do. Here's our why . . . the cause we believe in. And here's how we do it." A company that empowers those they lead with the Watch one, Do one, Teach one, mentality. I believe one year of in-person, one-on-one, on-the-job coaching and training is worth more than the same amount paid over four years of a traditional education.

(Not that I'm against traditional education. I hope the Harvards of the world are still around when I'm ready to pursue my lifelong dream of becoming a neurologist. Or maybe a neurosurgeon. Or perhaps a cognitive neuroscientist. I predict I'll be in my mid-seventies by then.)

One of my favorite movie scenes is the one in *The Pursuit of Happyness* (2006) when Chris Gardner (played by Will Smith) has a brief conversation with a stockbroker. The broker has just pulled up in his Ferrari and as he drops coins in the meter, Chris says to him, "I got two questions for you: What do you do? And how do you do it?"

The broker smiles, pointing to the skyscraper in front of him, "I'm a stockbroker."

I love how the scene plays out. Chris looks up, squints into the sun, and with a tinge of daunted hope in his voice, asks, "Stockbroker? Oh. Had to go to college to be a stockbroker, huh?"

"You don't have to. You have to be good with numbers, and good with people." He gives Chris a vote of confidence as he looks him in the eye and cuffs him on the shoulder. "That's it."

It's an inciting incident, a turning point, for Chris. He knows he doesn't want his son to feel the pain he felt as a child growing up not knowing his father. And he knows the path he's on won't break the generational poverty and abandonment.

He knows he's good with numbers. He recounts to his son on the way to daycare that his nickname as a child was Ten-Gallon Head because he was smart back then. And he knows he's good with people—his work as a salesman has trained him.

He decides to go for it.

His application is accepted and he begins a six-month internship as a stockbroker.

The unfolding story is one of determination and grit. It's my go-to movie whenever I'm facing something that feels impossible.

But the two questions that are embedded as life mantras on my list of go-to questions are, "What do you do? And how do you do it?"

Those questions are a slightly different version of, "Why are you the way you are?"

And I've been asking them for as long as I can remember. Two sentences formed my belief system about learning. When I was eleven years old, I read a story written by a teenager in a magazine that was running a contest for young writers. And, while I don't remember the name of the writer or what the story was about, I can still picture those two sentences written into her bio at the bottom of the page. "Whenever someone is better than you at something, don't be jealous of them. Learn from them."

Learn from them. Be teachable. Be coachable.

I met with a life coach the other day. The representative on the phone said they require three important elements from the clients they coach: 1) there has to be a gap between where you are and where you want to be—a vision and a goal you want to achieve; 2) you need to have reasons for why you want to achieve that goal; and 3) you must be coachable.

Those three elements sound like why students pay tens of thousands of dollars to go to school. Now, consider this: life coaches and business coaches typically help their students (aka, clients) get results in twelve to eighteen months.

On the television reality show, Shark Tank, contestants pitch their business ideas to successful business moguls in the hopes that they'll get investment capital. But they get something much more valuable than money . . . If one of the "sharks" agrees to fund the contestant's venture, they also agree to mentor and coach them in their business. I'd go on that show just to pitch an idea and get one of them to mentor me. Never mind the money. The coaching is priceless.

As for my idea of investing $212,000 per child for a four-year, university-level training in one year? I'm already making a list of people whom I respect and trust as mentors and coaches. Many of them are mentioned in this book. There are many more whose stories I didn't tell. People who I'll send my mentorship and coaching proposal to who are living selfless, impacting, visionary legacies . . .

And this also got me thinking. What about the legacy *I'm* living today? Am I the kind of person who could be trusted to mentor and coach another person's progeny? Could I be trusted with a corporate entity's employees? And if not, what am I doing to *become* someone whose integrity, fortitude, selflessness, service, and vision is making a positive difference in the lives of those I impact? Those are loaded questions. And they ought to be. At the end of the day, we get to look back and survey the legacy in our wake. Did I communicate with love? Did I build a culture of honor in the spaces I occupied? Did I act as a multiplier, giving others an opportunity to share their ideas and solve problems? Or did I act as a diminisher, rushing in to do things for people because I want it done my way? Did I encourage exploration and experimentation? Did I invite candor and provide a safe place where people can share openly and honestly?

Did I catch any vision leaks and give fresh encouragement and insight into where we are in achieving the organization's vision? Have I helped those around me in their personal and professional development? Did I listen? Did I ask great questions? Did I approach challenges with a solution-oriented mentality? Did I laugh with people?

Did I live a legacy today that values the adventure of living? Regarding the team, what did we learn? Where did we grow? What did we try that was new, maybe difficult, and maybe even scary? Did we fail at anything? Did we acknowledge and celebrate any successes?

These are the questions rattling through my brain. They're questions that demand answers to help me write a purposeful, meaningful narrative for the legacy I want to live. They're questions prompted from a heart of gratitude and the desire to honor the truth of *I am enough*. To live from a place of abundance and the dream of helping others live inspired and passionate. To abound in hope.

I know people whose lives answer these questions with integrity and extraordinary impact as they lead those in their influence. They're not perfect. And that's another reason I listen to their advice and wisdom—because they're real. They share where they went wrong and what they learned. They share their journey, with its' failures and scrapes and bruises and scars. Then when I find myself in a pit, their response is, "We've all been there."

Really? You, too?

Yes.

Several months ago, my son, Isaiah, now nineteen years old, contacted one of his mentors (who mentors from "afar" through his books and podcasts). The administrative assistant emailed Isaiah back with, "[Mentor's name] would be happy to schedule a call with you. You can schedule through his website and pay the $2,000 for a sixty-minute coaching call at checkout." Isaiah told me, "Well, I guess I'll have to save up and then schedule the call."

This is the same son who asked me a cage-rattling question one day as we were going through stacks of old papers and notes that I've kept for way too long. (In fact, I used to believe I was a classic paper hoarder. But now I'm organizing ideas buried within the quotes and notes, searching for revolutionary ideas. I'll keep you posted.)

"Mom, do you want your legacy to your children to be things . . . or values?"

I stopped and looked up at him. The beauty of raising cool people is that they call you on your stuff (no pun intended) later.

This whole living your legacy idea . . . The second definition of "legacy" in the American Heritage Dictionary is, "Something handed down from an ancestor or predecessor or from the past."

Like the wake left behind a boat as it moves across the water, our lives are leaving a wake. At the end of the day, what are the virtues and values I've left in my wake? What is the story I told? And when I begin again tomorrow, what is the vision for the legacy I want to live? The culture I want to cultivate?

Every single person has a unique contribution to make to the world around them. We need to listen to our heart and pursue the dreams and passions that cause us to love bigger, bolder, more fiercely and fearlessly. When we honor our calling and purpose for being here, we'll inspire others to do the same. People like the teachers I met in the African Bush, (who inspired *me* by jolting me from complacency), who are changing the world—one student at a time.

Have you seen the Forbes "Best Places to Work" list? The common denominators are places where leaders are committed to training and developing their people. The best companies have vision, uphold a core set of values, and are led by transformational leaders—equipping their people to grow, empowering them, and releasing them to be the best versions of themselves, operate in their strengths, and make a positive difference. To do their best work. The best companies are supportive and caring, deliberately creating cultures where employees feel like family.

Not surprisingly, these are the companies that hold reputations—legacies—for excellent customer service.

Imagine if we intentionally thought out the story we want to tell through the culture of our marriage and home life? What might it be like if we envisioned a storyboard based on timeless principles and our core set of values? How might our own commitment to character-training and discipline, based on who we want to be, ripple from our dining room tables to the frontlines wherever we serve and lead? And what if the cultures in our boardrooms and offices and factory floors ignited a spirit of excellence and passion, purpose and *fun*, that splashed over into our personal lives at home? What if we were all so intent on investing in people and relationships, that the resulting cultures spurred creativity and innovation in processes and tasks?

What if we found ways to connect and engage deeper, more wholehearted?

Might we discover *freedom* as we get out of our comfort zones, run with endurance, and push past our limits?

We're made for this. To know who we are and that our story and the future story we're creating matters . . . to *purpose* to live beyond ourselves, passionate, investing deeply in a legacy that's eternal:

Relationships.

ACKNOWLEDGMENTS

This book represents a collective force of incredible thought leaders and influencers who have invested in my life. I am honored to ride on the coattails of their legacies.

~~*~*

The saying is true: you are the average of the five people you surround yourself with. And while I have hundreds of five's, I continue to be awe-inspired by the five people I get to do life with on the most intimate level:

To the love of my life, LeRoy. Thank you for believing in me when I didn't believe in myself. For praying over me at night even though I'm usually fast asleep before you complete your first sentence. For being mindful of the schedule in the midst of my chaotic spontaneity. For being patient like Ricky when I get myself into Lucy-like predicaments. Thank you for putting feet to a long—very long—list of dreams. If it weren't for you, my ideas would still be just ideas, including this book. Not only are you a dream come true, but it is one of my greatest joys in life to be by your side as we live this adventure of turning our dreams into reality together.

To my gurus of play and celebration and courageous exploits, Eli, Isaiah, Ezekiel, and Israel. The four of you continue to inspire and humble me with your hilarity, insight, vision, and passion. You four are God's affirmation of His infinite grace to and extravagant love for me. I love being your mom.

Eli, thank you for showing me what it looks like to be bold, take risks, and live with conviction. Your selfless leadership, generosity of spirit, and love for people inspire me to live open-hearted and expectant.

Isaiah, I love your ability to cause me to laugh until tears and snot cascade down my face. I'm also incredibly grateful for your deep insights, insatiable curiosity, and passionate pursuit of more excellence. Thank you for teaching me to notice the miracles strewn throughout the journey.

Ezekiel, I appreciate how you engage people, genuinely interested in what causes them to feel loved and valued. Through your example of thoughtfulness, you teach me to go the extra mile, be conscientious, and notice details for the sake of honoring others.

Martha Rae Lovewell (aka Israel), girl, I love how your passion and zeal for living full on, no holds barred, is as large as a nation. Your tears over injustice and determination to be part of solutions spur me to stay the course and expand my hope like no other. I'm grateful for your unwavering enthusiasm to try new things, challenge the status quo, and seize the next adventure.

To all four of you, I'm following your lead.

~~*~*

Mom and Dad, I love you and I'm forever grateful for you and the way you raised me. For endless, unstructured time filled with reading books and exploring the town on my bicycle. Who would have guessed that all those hours making up stories and using my imagination to create my own fun would be the backdrop to this incredible life as an adult? Thank you for taking us on adventures and for traveling with us. Thank you for teaching me to love words and story. Thank you for fostering the relationship between us and our grandparents. And thank you for being lenient all those times growing up when I wouldn't stay in the playroom, instead opting to sit in to listen to the adult conversations. You all were far more interesting than games and toys.

Catherine, I have adored you from the moment Mom and Dad brought you home from the hospital, placed you in my arms, and told me, "Here's your baby sister. You get to help take care of her." Your friendship is one of God's greatest gifts to me. Aaron, I love that you are an amazing husband to my sister and father to your family. You two are role models and mentors—in marriage, parenting, taking risks... Your "less talk, more action" approach to life is a beacon for others to follow. We're all more daring and bold because of you.

Tim, how cool is it that you are nine years younger than me and yet you're one of my best friends and biggest mentors. Thank you for all the encouragement you constantly give me—especially the more audacious the idea, the more apt you are to laugh that laugh of yours and ask, "Why not?!" Tyann, I love that you are my sister-in-love. Thank you for demonstrating what it looks like to live life messy and beautiful. For teaching me to see life as a canvas and to boldly throw paint on it—that we can always change the color later. I love you.

Rebekah, I love you.

Aunt Kathy and Uncle Jake, thank you for being bold and courageous. Your extravagant love changed my husband's destiny and impacted the man he's become. Thank you for always being there for us, for supporting us and speaking hope into our marriage and our parenting. I'm grateful for the innumerable home cooked meals in which you not only poured your labor of love into, but you taught me to appreciate the finer side of cuisine. And I'm thankful for the hours upon hours of conversation—and perspective—you've blessed me with over the last twenty-three years.

Merilee Moser, thank you for taking me to my very first writer's conference. It was there that not only did I get to meet one of my heroes, Ann Kiemel-Anderson, but I awakened to the idea that my words didn't have to stay hidden in my journals. Talk about a legacy... it was because you ran the nanny agency and found me my dream job in Spokane, that I met LeRoy. Look at the ripples of your legacy!

Niki Anderson, for the last seventeen years, your persistent mentoring, coaching, and teaching have stirred the writing embers. Thank you for investing in me not only as a writer, but helping me be a better wife and mom. Thank you teaching me the value of "15 minutes."

Ronna Snyder, your passion and unshakable belief that I had a book inside me has been a force that has driven me to the finish line. From that first moment when I timidly asked if I could meet with you to talk about writing, to the evening you invited me out to your sweet country cabin and treated me as though I was already a bestselling author... your support and constant encouragement has helped me keep putting one word in front of the other.

Laurie Klein, I'll never forget the time a handful of us writers convened at Christine's house on the South Hill. We had just settled in, when someone asked how you were doing. I love how you blurted out, "I'm considering taking up knitting. Perhaps it'll prove to be more lucrative and surely it'll be easier." Laughter rippled through the room. And I thought, *well then, if someone like Laurie can keep at this writing thing and still make light of it, even when—or because?—it's hard, then I guess I'll stick with it, too.* And I don't think I ever thanked you proper when you bought me dinner and invited me to sit next to you while at the writer's conference. I remember thinking, *this is who I want to be like when I'm a successful author like Laurie.*

Bethany Schafer, thank you for sharing your presence with me. For all those afternoons when we met to read each other's writing and offer feedback. You taught me to take the craft of writing words and transform them into art. You showed me how to paint with words and how to pen soul onto paper. Thank you for teaching me not to "eddy"—in writing or life.

Ruth McHaney Danner, thank you for facilitating the South Hill writer's critique group. Your soft-spoken-yet-direct approach taught me to value the impact of the written word. To be professional and faithful at all times. Your direct and helpful feedback made me a braver writer.

Amy Strebel, you're one of the few people on earth whose soul is so intimately intertwined with mine. I love that our story spans 32 years. That's a lot of coffee over countless hours of conversation. Thank you for believing the best in me, for knowing how far to push and trusting the elongated pause. Every cliché phrase to tell you how much I love you... comes up short to describe my depth of love for you. Darren, thank you for daring me.

To Michael Baxter, who always looked for ways to make the journey more fun for all of us. The legacy you lived made you a legend, my friend. You are missed.

Penny Kafflen, DeAnn Sylvia, Cathy Rojan, Laurie Thomson, Anna Pemberton, Laura Bubna, thank you for including me in your life. For letting me incessantly ask questions. For meeting with me at five o'clock in the morning for 78 Wednesdays (Laurie). For numerous coffee dates. For sharing your stories, including what worked and what didn't. For being there for the births of my babies and for inviting me and other moms into your home to "discuss whatever was on our minds" (Laura). For listening to my self-righteous rants and then gently nudging me to examine my own heart. Your mentoring and coaching helped me grow in integrity, change the storyline to be congruent with my vision, and become a more effective, impactful, and visionary leader. I'm forever grateful for your influence in my life.

To Chandler Bolt and the team at Self Publishing School, thank you for putting together a world class experience where writing hopefuls take elusive dreams and turn them into published successes.

Steve Roller, your superpowers are your authenticity and ability to care deeply about people right where they're at while at the same time challenging them to go further than they thought they could go. I'm fortunate and blessed to have you as a business coach and friend.

Ramy, thank you for coaching me through the writing process. Your oversight, encouragement, and forthright feedback held me accountable to my own ideals, helped me achieve massive breakthroughs, and got me to the finish line with the first draft. I wouldn't be writing an Acknowledgement section in a book if it weren't for you.

Spencer Borup and Mandy Baxter, you're golden. Your edits have not only transformed this manuscript, but my heart has changed in the process. Thank you for consistently challenging me to ask myself, "What is this for?" Every story, every paragraph, every sentence came under your scrutiny and for that, I'm deeply grateful. Thank you for seeing potential in my writing and for helping me think deeper, trust my heart, and write with congruency, authenticity, and purpose throughout.

Austin Netzley, I'm honored and grateful to be part of your Mastermind Group. Thank you for guiding me through the process of preparing for and launching this book. Thank you for mentoring me on this entrepreneurship journey. Your insights and constant encouragement are invaluable.

Jeri Hawkins and Sarah Kortright, thank you for starting the writer's group in Spangdahlem and thank you for inviting me to join you. Meeting with you and hearing your progress on the manuscripts you were working on, fueled my dreams of someday finishing a book, too. Thank you for opening your lives. For your vulnerability. For your inspiration.

Mary DeMuth and the writers I met in Switzerland, thank you for a week of wisdom, knowledge, insights and an outpouring of faith, hope and love. It is a rare opportunity to connect so intimately with other artists who are, as Theodore Roosevelt wrote, daring greatly. I'm inspired by the impact you're making in the world, by your prayers, and by your vision to love deeply whoever intersects your path.

Donna Barker, you're a reminder of the gifts that come as a result of staying open, reaching out, and living wholehearted. Thank you for demonstrating what it means to show up in the world honest, true, authentic, vulnerable, and courageous. Thank you for asking questions that challenge me. Thank you for listening. I'm grateful to be on this journey with you.

Karamel McCoy, Israel Olson, Ebony Stepp, and Leah Cymonne, I'm honored to be part of your Mastermind Group. Thank you for seeing more in me than I dare to see in myself. Thank you for challenging me to go further, not settle, and give more. Your fierce love and your desire to help people live wholehearted ignites creativity, courage, and faith in those whose lives you influence.

I stand amazed and deeply grateful for the relentless and boundless love of Abba Father God.

About the Author

Sharon Olson is an author, speaker, thought leader, visionary, entrepreneur, and mentor with an unshakable optimism regarding the remarkable narratives we can live in our personal lives and businesses. Inspired by dreamers, artists, scientists, and luminaries, she holds to the conviction that we don't have to settle for antiquated, broken, or mediocre systems. She's a relentless Possibilitarian on a mission to help leaders maximize their purpose and potential. As a leading-learner, she's on a quest to discover what it means to abound in hope, believe anything is possible, and love with wild, reckless abandonment.

When she and her husband, LeRoy, aren't traveling the world, they make their home in Spokane, Washington. They have three grown sons, Eli, Isaiah, and Ezekiel, and a daughter, Israel. Get in touch with her at www.sharonannolson.com.

www.ingramcontent.com/pod-product-compliance
Lightning Source LLC
Chambersburg PA
CBHW070315190526
45169CB00005B/1634